The Call of the Woods

AN EDGAR GUEST COLLECTION

Written and compiled by Jenny Phillips
with contributions from Rebecca Borger and Maurianne Baker

Cover design by Tina DeKam
Inside illustrations by Kessler Garrity

© 2020 Jenny Phillips | goodandbeautiful.com

This document may be copied or printed for use within your own family once downloaded directly from goodandbeautiful.com. However, this document may not be shared with others in any way.

Printed in Canada

Chapter 1

An Introduction

It's wonderful when poems bring you delight as you read them. It's wonderful when poems fill your mind with beautiful images and messages. Nevertheless, it is *astounding* when a poem stays with you for years to come and changes the way you act and think.

This is exactly how poems by Edgar Guest have affected my own life. For example, years after reading a poem by Edgar Guest, I had a newborn baby that cried for hours a day and hardly slept at night. As I exhaustedly took care of my baby, lines from Edgar Guest's poem "Baby Feet" kept flooding my mind:

Tell me, what is half so sweet
As a baby's tiny feet

Those lines repeatedly changed my mood from frustration to appreciation as I cared for my precious baby.

In addition, I often hear lines from Edgar Guest's poem "Silent" when I see flowers or magnificent trees, and my mind is turned to gratitude and deeper joy.

Too well I know what accident
And chance and force disclose
To think blind fury could invent
The beauty of a rose.

I'm not alone in being changed by Edgar Guest's poetry. ESPN.com explains how Guest's poetry affected football player Kordell Stewart, who had a successful 11-year NFL career:

> In *Truth*, Stewart's 2016 autobiography, he describes a particularly ugly scene after a game in Pittsburgh. "As I walked off the field and into the tunnel," he wrote,

"someone threw a cup full of beer at my head that gushed into my eyes. I looked up. A man looked me dead in the eyes and yelled '[a derogatory term]!'" Stewart walked away. Somewhere in the back of his mind was the Edgar Albert Guest poem "See It Through." He had memorized it growing up and took comfort in the words "You may fail, but you may conquer/See it through!"[1]

When you're up against a trouble,
Meet it squarely, face to face;
Lift your chin and set your shoulders,
Plant your feet and take a brace.
When it's vain to try to dodge it,
Do the best that you can do;
You may fail, but you may conquer,
See it through!

Black may be the clouds about you
And your future may seem grim,
But don't let your nerve desert you;
Keep yourself in fighting trim.
If the worst is bound to happen,
Spite of all that you can do,
Running from it will not save you,
See it through!

Even hope may seem but futile,
When with troubles you're beset,
But remember you are facing
Just what other men have met.
You may fail, but fall still fighting;
Don't give up, whate'er you do;
Eyes front, head high to the finish.
See it through!

Kordell Stewart and I join millions of people who have been influenced by Guest in emphatic

---

1. Steve Wulf, "Who's Got Next? The Four Athletes Who Appeared on Our First Cover," September 10, 2019, https://www.espn.com/espn/story/_/id/27500438/got-next-four-athletes-appeared-our-first-cover.

ways. His sagacious gift with words and his understanding of how to connect to the cares and joys of everyday people gave him the name the People's Poet and made him one of the most successful poetry writers in modern history, even though other poets of his day didn't take his poetry seriously.

Truly one of the most prolific poets of all time, Guest wrote well over 11,000 poems during his lifetime. His works appeared daily in hundreds of newspapers across America, making his name known in most homes in the country.

The following quotes give insight into the impact of Guest's poetry:

> "Such poetry as that of Edgar A. Guest has the ring of genuineness, for it is based on a deep, abiding faith in human nature—an essential goodness and lovableness. It is this human quality in his verse that has made Mr. Guest one of the favorite poets of America." —R. Marshall[2]

> "He is both wise and witty; he is the best serum I know against pessimistic philosophy, indigestion, and bad temper." —Rev. Dr. Cavanaugh, President of the University of Notre Dame[3]

> "He had what every person must have who goes far in the education of his fellow-man—enthusiasm, enthusiasm that no worry, no interruption, or disquieting news can take the edge from." —Edward H. Cotton[4]

---

2. R. Marshall, *Edgar Guest: A Biographical Sketch* (n.p.: Reilly & Lee, 1920).
3. As quoted in Royce Howes and John S. Knight, *Edgar A. Guest: A Biography* (n.p.: Literary Licensing, 2011).
4. Edward H. Cotton, "Edgar A. Guest, the Fireside Poet," *The Christian Register,* December 7, 1922, 1161–62.

Perhaps Edgar Guest was beloved by people because he himself had a deep love for all people. He said, "I like people wherever I see them, whatever they are doing, whoever they are."[5]

Proverbs 13:20 states: "He that walketh with wise men shall be wise." As you journey through this book, feasting on the wisdom and wit of Edgar Guest, I hope you will be one of the people who becomes just a little better and one whose soul expands just a little more for having experienced the works of Edgar Guest.

Edward H. Cotton said it best: "Men are better after hearing Edgar Guest or reading his poems. . . . Fortunate are we who find the road somewhat rough and blinding in having such companions for the journey as Edgar Guest."[6]

Edgar once wrote a poem titled "My Creed," which described the beliefs that drove his actions and the principles behind his poetry. As you study the poems in this book, you will see the foundations in the principles of this poem.

My Creed

To live as gently as I can;
To be, no matter where, a man;
To take what comes of good or ill
And cling to faith and honor still;
To do my best, and let that stand
The record of my brain and hand;
And then, should failure come to me,
Still work and hope for victory.

To have no secret place wherein
I stoop unseen to shame or sin;
To be the same when I'm alone
As when my every deed is known;

---

5. Edgar A. Guest, as quoted in Cotton, "Edgar A. Guest."
6. Cotton, "Edgar A. Guest."

To live undaunted, unafraid
Of any step that I have made;
To be without pretense or sham
Exactly what men think I am.

To leave some simple mark behind
To keep my having lived in mind;
If enmity to aught I show,
To be an honest, generous foe,
To play my little part, nor whine
That greater honors are not mine.
This, I believe, is all I need
For my philosophy and creed.

Chapter 2

Early Life and Fatherhood

Interestingly, Edgar Guest was born in Birmingham, England, in August 1881. However, the majority of his life was spent in the United States as a US citizen. After a failed business in 1890, his father, Edwin Guest, moved to relocate his entire family—which included Edgar; his mother, Julia; his eldest brother, Sidney; his sister, Florence; his next-older brother, Percy; and finally, the baby of the family, Harry. Edgar was the next to youngest in the family, older only than Harry.

Edwin chose the United States for a fresh start and, in particular, he chose Detroit, Michigan, because the Guests had family there. Edgar's father first traveled overseas with Percy to establish a place to bring his young, growing family. In 1891, the rest of the family traveled to join them. Edgar was nine and a half. The family would settle in and build a life that would root them deeply in Detroit, Michigan.

An introduction to Edgar Guest best begins with the impact of his beloved parents, for whom he would express gratitude and affection for all of his life. Edgar Guest was closely connected to and deeply affected by both of his parents. They had a great influence on his life, and he carried that forward both into his future and into the foundations of his own family as a grown man.

His mother, Julia Guest, had the most profound influence on Edgar. Her careful nurture of his faith in God laid the foundation for his future belief. He credited her spiritual guidance as being the true source of all that was good, true, and prosperous in his life; indeed, Edgar Guest offered all the honor and glory for everything good in his life back to the work and provision of God. His mother provided spiritual teaching and direction that formed the bedrock of his faith, which would carry him through the whole of his life, blessings and trials together. Of his mother, he said, "She taught me to believe in God. Without that religious belief which she impressed upon me, I am sure I would not be where I am today."

Julia Guest was also deeply connected to Edgar through their mutual love of literature, books, and words. She lived many more years after Edwin to bless and add to Edgar's life. Some of Edgar's earliest memories were formed at his mother's knee as she read aloud to him from the rocking chair in his grandmother's home in England while they waited to journey to America. This experience fueled Edgar's and his mother's joint love of stories and words. Edgar absorbed the full range of emotions and also a wonderful appreciation and aptitude for humor that would stay with him all his life. Their warm, mutual interest in the many great works of literature closed the span of years between Julia Guest and young Edgar. Both possessed a deep, instinctive love of good literature and most especially of good poetry. He said of his mother, "It must be from her that I drew my immense love of reading." This love was reflected in his own substantial and beautiful library as a grown man as well as in his sense of words, rhythm, and rhyme, and in his aptitude to put it together in beloved verse. Most of all, Julia Guest loved Shakespeare. Quite naturally, Edgar came to know and love him too. Edgar became so familiar with the plays that he could aptly interject a Shakespearean line for any occasion—and especially wield the lines with humor. However, it was vitally important to Edgar his whole life through that he never use his humor or his words to hurt another person. He actively and consciously chose never to employ words to wound or tear down others.

Julia Guest not only loved literature, she was brave and courageous, too. Perhaps it was from Julia Guest that Edgar gained the strength of character that would inform him for all of his life as he built a name and legacy for himself. Facing the unknown, Julia Guest moved her large family from England to a foreign land to begin again in support of her husband. She left her parents, siblings, country, and all that she knew. At one point, Edgar said in tribute to his parents, "I am not sure I could have done it. But my father and mother did. And, because they did, all that has enriched my life was made possible."

Edgar's father died when Edgar was just sixteen. Edwin Guest only lived a few short years after their move across the ocean from England to America. Yet, his impact on his son was immeasurable. Indeed, his father's powerful influence formed the basis for Edgar's own heart for fatherhood as an adult. This influence is clearly seen in the two short books by Edgar Guest included here in this chapter: *My Job As a Father* and *What My Father Did for Me*, both written in 1923 when Guest was 42 years old.

My Job As a Father

My boy, Bud, is ten years old and I've just passed forty. I have always taken his presence in the family circle seriously. I have held myself in a general way responsible for his welfare and his future, but not until recently did it dawn upon me just what a man-sized job I have on my hands.

Bud has graduated from his babyhood into his boyhood. In a way he has quit his mother's knee and turned to me for counsel and comradeship.

Up to a few months ago his place at the table was by his mother. She prepared his food, arranged the napkin under his chin, and taught him what table manners a pink-cheeked, healthy, and roguish lad could assimilate.

Then one night she made a startling discovery. He was getting too big for her to handle. He was developing—as all boys develop—certain traits and manners which are the bane and the chagrin of all fond mothers. And she was not getting anywhere with her tutoring.

So she transferred him to me. I am supposed to keep watch over him and do the correcting. He is to learn from me what is proper to do. His future table manners are in my hands.

Since then I have been doing a lot of thinking. My job as Bud's father goes beyond table manners. I have been wondering lately just what I must do to be successful as his dad. What would it mean to me if I should turn out a failure in that respect?

I have a number of tasks to do, all of which I should like to do well. To be a failure in any one of them would be disappointing; yet I could bear that without whimpering if I were sure that I had not failed the boy.

I have known of a number of wealthy men who were not successful as fathers. They made money rapidly; their factories were marvels of organization; their money investments were sound and made with excellent judgment, and their contributions to public service were useful and willingly made. All this took time and thought. At the finish there was a fortune on the one hand—and a worthless and dissolute son on the other. Why? Too much time spent in money-making implies too little time spent with the boy.

Had someone, when the child was a youngster romping on the floor, come to any one of those fathers and offered him a million dollars for the lad he would have spurned the offer and kicked the proposer out of doors. Had someone offered him ten million dollars in cash for the privilege of making a drunkard out of his son, the answer would have been the same. Had someone offered to buy from him for a fortune the privilege of playing with the boy, of going on picnics and fishing trips and outings, and being with him a part of every day, he would have refused the proposition without giving it a second thought.

Yet that is exactly the bargain those men made, and which many men are still making. They are coining their lives into fortunes and automobile factories and great industries, but their boys are growing up as they may. These men probably will succeed in business; but they will be failures as fathers. To me it seems that a little less industry and a little more comradeship with the boy is more desirable.

Not so much of me in the bank, and more of me and of my best in the lad, is what I should like to have to show at the end of my career.

To be the father of a great son is what I should call success.

Naturally, I should like to have much to leave my boy, but if I could have my choice I should prefer to leave him so equipped for life that he would need no man's help. Better than money would be to leave him self-reliant and manly and able to earn his own way in the world.

This is what I conceive my job to be.

The problem is not easy to work out. In the first place I must make myself Bud's best friend. If I am to succeed in my job as his dad I must have his confidence, not some of his confidence, but all of it. I must be the one he will turn to first when he is in trouble. There must be no one else—no uncle, no neighbor, no acquaintance—to whom he would sooner go. He must not be afraid of me. It is therefore not enough for me to tell Bud that I am his best friend; he must know that for himself. He must feel that no matter what may happen I am to be depended on. Of all his companions I must be first.

This means that I've got to make myself worthy of his confidence. This is no one-sided trust. It is a mutual arrangement.

I can't be a "shut-up" father, and hope to win.

I've watched the "shut-up" fathers and seen the

results. The loud-voiced, strident and irritable type, which imagines verbal abuse and parental intolerance to be correction and training, is doomed to failure. "Shut-up," is a terse and emphatic command, and the child eventually obeys it to the letter. He may disobey all other regulations and orders, but when told to "shut up" often enough he will do that consciously and subconsciously. He will shut up within himself all the many little treasures of his confidence, which he should be happy to give out and which his parents would be happy to possess.

One of the chief dangers as I see it is the tendency to expect from children the same wise reasoning which adults are supposed to practice. We think we are punishing them for their faults, when the fact is we are punishing them because at nine or ten or eleven or twelve years they have not acquired the experienced wisdom of their elders. We tell them they should have known better. At their age we did not ourselves know better, and at nine years no child will ever know better. To expect too much from a boy is apt to lead to punishing him merely for being nine years old.

The task is one which seems to call for all the thought and patience I can bring to it. There are so many phases to be considered. Success as a father cannot wholly be written in kindness. Failure almost certainly awaits the over-indulgent father. To gratify a child's every whim is the easy thing to do. It is what the heart prompts every parent to do.

Most of us who are fathers now have said to ourselves more than once that our children should have some of the pleasures of childhood which were denied to us. With us who went early to work, whose parents battled for the comforts which they could supply, whose boyhood was spent between school and the newspaper route or the errand-running for the neighborhood druggist, this tendency predominates. The toys we went without and the pleasures we lost, our children shall have. Yet in this dream of kindness lies great danger.

Better for us were the hardships we endured. There is more hope for the busy boy than the idle one. The parents who let their children eat more candy than is good for them because they plead for it cause pain and suffering where they hoped only to give pleasure. So on to the end of the chapter. Over-indulgence is Folly's broadest road.

I know one wealthy couple who have reared an only son with rare judgment. Both the father and mother had known hardships in their youth. The boy was born before fortune began to smile upon them. Within a few years riches came to them as a flood. There was nothing money could buy that that boy could not have.

One little illustration will suffice to show the tact and wisdom of the mother. There came a winter when the boys were wearing leather gauntlets.

The son wanted a pair.

"You may have them," said the mother.

"I can get a dandy pair for eight dollars," said the boy.

The mother shook her head. "Eight dollars is too much to pay for gauntlets," she said. "You may have a two-dollar pair, like those all the other boys are wearing."

It wasn't the price she was worrying about; it was the effect of too much money upon her boy. That son has come through an avenue of riches unspoiled. He has learned the value of money and what is more, has kept the friendships of his boyhood.

There comes often the time when it is easier to give than to refuse. It takes time to explain; and it is often difficult to do. Tears flow quickly from little eyes. Whims ungratified are hard to forget. To refuse what you can afford seems strangely stern. Many a father has given, only to get the child out of his way—to find later that the son has "gone out of his way" forever.

I know that I must not be over-indulgent. Mother laughs at the way I give in to Bud. How to give in *wisely* is my problem. To fail him there might cost him greatly later on.

We have certain regulations. Bedtime for Bud is eight-thirty o'clock during the school week. The picture show is not permitted until Friday evening, except on certain special occasions. At times this rule seems hard, but it is adhered to. However, there are no tantrums about it. Bud and I have talked this over too many times for any misunderstanding to exist. We have reasoned it out.

At meal times we talk the day over. What has interested him interests me, and what has puzzled him I try to make clear. He is not allowed to monopolize the conversation, but he may share in it. When guests are at the table the same condition is observed. We do not embarrass him with too much instruction or rob him of his ease with too much restraint. His table manners are not forced and unnatural. Formality may properly be required of an adult, but a healthy boy is entitled to some leeway.

My job as a father is a day and night task, and involves not only Bud but me also. It is twofold in its obligation. I feel that I owe to him the best I can do with my strength. I cannot be a good father—and a poor citizen. I cannot be true to him—and false to my neighbors. I cannot be a cheat downtown—and a symbol of honor at home. If I am careless in my business, I shall be careless with him, too.

This means that I must try to succeed for his sake. If I have gained his confidence I must also—in order to keep that confidence—gain his pride and respect. Not to do my own work to the best of my ability would be unfair to him. He is a partner in all that can come to me. If I lose, he loses. If shame and disgrace come to me, he suffers, too, and I have failed him as a father.

By all the laws of inheritance he is entitled to a clean name. I may not be able to leave him wealth or social position, but it is within my power to leave him that. This is an obligation which lies upon me, even when I am not with him.

But how much of my time must be given to Bud? To what is he entitled by right? I think he is entitled to my companionship. The difficulty lies in the conflict between what seems business necessity and his demands. It is not always possible to go pleasure-seeking with him. There are times when little of the day can be spent with him. Lately we have been separated for whole weeks at a time. The demands upon me have grown to an appalling extent. My duty to the public and my duty as a father cannot be reconciled. He has reached that age where he needs more of me, but more and more I am being called away from home. Yet if he is to know me and if I am to know him, we must be together.

I think that my job as a father requires a complete intimacy with my boy. I must not only know him thoroughly but I must know his playmates, too.

This means that I cannot walk by the vacant lot where they are playing. If it's a baseball game I must take part in it. I took part in what I thought was my last ball game before Bud was born. I noticed then that I was slowing down. I couldn't get the grounders out of the dirt the way I used to, and the play at second base found me dodging danger rather than meeting it. My right arm, never strong, couldn't get the ball across the diamond, and I decided that age had called me to the bench. But I am playing ball again. Just a few minutes ago I came in from a game. I was busy on this article when he called:

"Dad, come on and peg me a few, will you?"

This was a morning set aside for this particular task. My first impulse was to refuse his request.

"Aw, gee!" he exclaimed. "You're always working when I want to play."

So I went out to peg him a few. Now I thought

I knew that boy. I fancied I could tell anyone all about him. Yet it had been almost a year since I had tossed a baseball to him.

"Is that the swiftest you can throw?" he asked with a grin.

"Do you want them faster?" I asked.

"Sure, burn 'em in!" he cried, and the old right arm went to work. To my surprise he could handle his mitt with ease and grace. He was not afraid of the ball and he caught what little speed I have left without flinching. To know a boy you must play with him.

I have lost my skill with marbles. I know my knees and knuckles are no longer suited to the game. I had forgotten even the rules or the sort of contests we used to have, until the day he appeared with agates and "miggles," as he now calls them. To us of the old days they were "mibs."

But I have been down in the dirt with him, and down on the carpet with him; we've disputed shots together, and although he can out-shoot me I have demonstrated to him that I once was a boy and I once could play.

This, then, is the basis of our companionship. I am his dad, but I have been myself a boy like him. There are times when this leads to difficulties. He is apt to expect too much of me in the way of agility and endurance. I can run one good race with him, but I cannot run the block six or seven times without fatigue. It is hard for him to understand that the boy in me is wearing a grown-up body.

From this play I have been able to learn much about him. I know the way he takes his defeats and his victories. I know the thoughts he thinks and the things he says in pleasure and in anger.

His education is also a part of my job. While I am a believer in the public school system of our country, and an admirer of the Detroit schools, my duty to him does not end at the schoolhouse door. Fine though his teachers are, there are many things they cannot teach him. His education cannot entirely be turned over to public officials. It is more my particular task than theirs. They may teach him the art of reading. I must teach him *what* to read, and *how*. So, many a night together we go rambling through the pages of Stevenson or Marryat or Tarkington, discussing the heroes and the desperadoes as we go. We know the good and the bad, and the difference between them. We know what is honest and what is dishonest, and why; what is good to do and what is wrong to do.

My job as his dad includes also an interest in his arithmetic and his geography. His monthly report cards are as important to me as the royalty statement of my publishers. I look upon it as an itemized account of my largest investment.

Here is a normal, healthy, roguish, fun-loving ten-year-old son, bearing my name and meaning more to me than my own selfish ambitions, bringing home an account of his month's labors. The figures written down are the judgments of his teachers upon his ability and his progress. It is more; it is a statement of my own endeavors in his behalf.

It is a good report, too. The figures show that in some subjects he is doing well; in others not so well; in one subject he is not making progress. There is one column that interests me more than all the others. It is marked "effort." I look to that and find that he marked "excellent," and I pat him on the back. He may not be doing perfect work, but he is trying. Excellent in arithmetic may be a mark of brilliance, but to be excellent in effort is a mark of character.

If I knew exactly what the future holds for him my job as his dad would be much easier. When he wants to learn how to throw a ball I can take him out and show him how it is done. There are things I can teach him which will be useful to his boyhood; there are things I shall teach him which shall be of benefit to his young manhood, but the goal of his destiny is not for me or anyone to know. It may be possible that great responsibilities await his growth. He may or may not rise to fame. However, I feel that I shall not have done my work well if the emergency of the future shall find him unprepared.

It is my duty to clothe him, feed him, and to give him a good home. I am not only morally bound to do that but legally also. But I can do all that and be a miserable failure as a father. I can robe him in the best of garments, and indulge him in every luxury, and pamper every whim, and at last leave him a fortune in gold and silver—and still be the cause of his ruin and the wrecker of his life.

For me to succeed as his father, *he* must succeed.

Unless my boy comes to manhood fit for the respect of his fellow men I shall have been a failure. The glory of our handiwork lies not in ourselves but in our sons. Greatness is not for us, but for those who follow us.

A few weeks ago a drunken and dissolute piece of humanity drifted into my office. He was pitiful to see. There was no place so low at which he was fit to serve. Incoherently he asked for money. I gave him a quarter and sent him shuffling on his way. It was an easy way to be rid of him, yet I was not so easily rid of him, either, for he lingered in my mind.

That wreck had once been a boy! Time was he was like Bud, just ten years old.

Would I, to write the world's greatest poem, or for an eternity of fame, have my boy sink so low? Suppose the choice were mine—a miserable outcast for a son, and fortune and high station for myself. Would I accept it? Or, to put it the other way around, what if I should come to greatness myself? What if, by dedicating all my time and all my strength and all my thought to what I could gain of glory and advantage in this world, I should at last achieve the very pinnacle of success? What moment of pleasure could it bring to me if Bud were lost in the decencies of life? Nothing else would be worth while if I should fail as a father.

Scarcely a day goes by that we do not witness this; fathers and mothers desolate and brokenhearted in the midst of plenty; not until too late did they discover that they were buying their own comfort at the expense of their boy.

My job as a father comes first. I do not belittle the value of money nor underestimate the worth of fame. He must be a happy man who rightly earns them both. The mistake is made in thinking them all-important.

Bud is calling to me now to play marbles again. He wants his dad and he needs him. In these few minutes on the ground I may teach him the way of honor. The stranger will play with him if I don't. The stranger *may* be good and fine and clean of speech, or he may not. I do not know. The stranger may teach him what I myself would teach, but I cannot be sure. The risk is too great to be run. I know that I shall never knowingly lead him astray. Boyhood is calling to its father, and boyhood cannot wait. If I lose this opportunity to be his comrade I may lose him forever.

 So out I go to play marbles.

The End

What My Father Did for Me

The people to whom we owe the most never remind us of our debts. They send no bills and they demand no settlement.

We receive joys beyond our present knowledge or understanding; wisdom is slipped into our mental pockets when our backs are turned; our feet are guided, and we know not how; we are shielded from harm and shame and misery; lifted over rough places and carried far on backs that may be wearier than our own; and it all is taken for granted; it all seems to be just a matter of course.

Then, some distant day when we are come to manhood and must stand alone before the world, we suddenly look back and discover how great were all those seemingly little things, and how courageous was the sacrifice which youth accepted unheedingly.

We are never furnished with a statement of such indebtedness. We discover it for ourselves—frequently when it is too late!

Why do I write this? Because I am thinking of one of the greatest of my own debts—the one to my father.

Lately I have been going back through the incidents of my life, trying to itemize the account. He isn't here to help me now; he kept no ledger in his dealings with me; he asked no return on his investment. I demanded much of him and he gave it all without one murmur of complaint.

Daily the debt grew, without my knowing it. In the first place, I didn't understand the kind of business my father was conducting in my behalf. Boys never do. I didn't know the extent of my drawing account with him, nor how diligently he was laboring to make my path the smooth one it has been.

I knew he was as fine a dad as any boy ever had—kind, cheerful, humorous, hard-working and patient; severe at times over my indifferent effort and boyish carelessness, but severe always with a kindly purpose, and very proud of his children whenever they did anything which seemed worthy. What I didn't know until too late was the depth of his wisdom and the magnitude of his sacrifice.

I was sixteen years of age when my father died, in the summer of 1897. My mother tells me that in his youth his hair was jet black. "The color of a raven's wing" was her poetic description of it. I can remember him only with gray hair which changed rapidly to white.

That snow-white glory fascinated me. It seemed to me to be the most beautiful hair I had ever seen on a man. He used to laugh at my adoration of it; and when, in my boyish way, I asked what made it so white he gave always the same terse answer: "It just faded."

I know now, what I never guessed back then—that white hair was the badge of my father's struggle for us all. He had suffered much, borne privations himself; stood to reverse; seen failure come, through no fault of his own; and finally, leaving the land of his birth and the friends of his lifetime, had come to the United States to start life anew, that his children should have their chance.

He died in his fifty-seventh year, respected by all who knew him, in debt to no man, and unstained by any act of shame or dishonor.

Once as a little chap I had a train of cars of which I was very fond. It was then my prize possession. A playmate who had come into the house wanted to play with it. I demurred. To me it seemed too precious to be risked in other hands. My father, who was reading in the next room, heard me refuse the boy's request for that train and track and called me to him.

"What does Bobby want?" he asked.

"To play with my train of cars," I said. "He'll break it, and I don't want him to have it."

"Get it out," said my father quietly. "Let him play with it."

I did as I was told, for he insisted always upon obedience. I remember that I thought my father unjust, and I know I did his bidding grudgingly. As I had feared, the boy broke my toy! It was a sobbing, heart-sick little fellow that my father called to him a second time.

"What are you crying about?" he asked.

"Bobby broke my train, as I knew he would if I let him have it," I said. He put down his newspaper and smiled. Then, taking me on his knee, he said very gently:

"You're not hurt at all. Bobby didn't kick you, or give you a black eye, or anything like that. Your fingers aren't cut and your legs are alright. I've looked you all over and I can't find that anything has happened that should make you cry."

Then he talked it all over with me. "Toys are made to give little boys pleasure," he said. "A toy which nobody ever uses is a wasted toy. If toys were never broken, never scratched and soiled, it would be a sign that no one had ever had any fun out of them. Now you had a train, and Bobby wanted to play with it. To have refused him that pleasure would have been selfish, and I don't want you to be selfish. I am sorry that Bobby broke it, but you shouldn't cry about it, for we can get more trains. It is easier to mend broken toys than it is to make an unselfish boy out of a selfish one."

That sounded like injustice to me. I still felt that I had been wronged in some way, but later I came to learn that it was this spirit of my father's which enabled him to face any material loss without whimpering. I owe to him the knowledge that in the mere possession of things there is no great happiness, and that there is no great sorrow in the loss of them. He taught me to use freely my possessions, especially if in the use of them I could bring joy to others.

Since then I have had the average man's run of hard luck; I've seen my precious little toys go all to smash; I've been given the worst of it at times; but so long as my losses have been *material* only I have tried not to "cry" over them. My father had taught me that they were not worth it.

The days of our comradeship began in Birmingham, England, where I was born. My memory begins in happy times before reverses brought heartache and trouble to us all.

I was my father's companion on his Sunday-morning walks. Holding his hand, I trudged gayly at his side up and down the hills of that city, learning from him then, unconsciously, much that was to serve me later on. I was too young to understand his purpose or to sense the process of his training. It is perfectly clear now—I was to see, with him, all that was good to see; and to learn, with him, all that was good to know.

A few weeks ago I received a letter from a kind old lady in Iowa. Something of mine had attracted her attention.

"You must be a very old man," she wrote. "You seem to have lived so much and to know what life is. How do you think of the things which touch us all so closely?"

I smiled as I read the letter, for I'm not so very old—unless you consider forty a tremendous weight of years. I'm still a kid, fond of play whenever I can get it. I think of myself only as a boy, and I do the same old willful, boyish things without ever pausing to think that I ought not to do them. I may grow up someday, but I don't want to. The only change that has come to me in the last twenty-five years that I can see is that I now wear long trousers. Oh, yes, there is one other—Father Time has made it necessary for me to shave every day.

But I know what it was that made that dear old lady in Iowa think me very old and wise. It was the voice of my father. I was but echoing in that bit of verse some lesson that he taught me. The rhyme may have been mine, but the thought was his. It was something that he gave me out of his wisdom on one of those wonderful walks of ours.

My father was the first to show me a business office. It was the one where he had been employed for many years as an expert accountant. I remember that I was curious, as all small boys are; but he was not content merely with gratifying my curiosity. He wanted me to learn the reason for all things in which I was interested.

Very proudly he led me into the office of the general manager, who took me on his knee and talked very kindly to me. I recall that Father seemed pleased with the way I answered the manager's questions.

There seems nothing extraordinary about such an event. It occurs in countless offices every day. Innumerable fathers have taken their little boys to the place of their employment, and the little boys, no doubt, have all enjoyed their experiences. But not every father thinks to make these happy little visits object lessons of real value.

On the way home Father talked to me of the people we had seen.

"That was a good man you met this morning, Sonny," he said to me. "Did you like him?"

When I replied that I did, he smiled and added: "Once he was a little boy, just like you; and when he first went to work he was cheerful and willing and obedient and did his best to please others. By and by he worked his way upward, until now he is in charge of the big factory you have just seen. Because he is a good man, people like him; because he has worked hard and faithfully and made the most of his opportunities, he has succeeded. Copy from good men and you will never go wrong."

This incident impressed me as my father intended it should. During our walks together he had a way of calling my attention to men he wanted me to know, and always he talked about them. He seemed to be acting as a pair of magnifying glasses for me, enlarging the good qualities of others that I might see them clearly. I never saw a great man without my father explaining to me why he was great, nor a bad man without being made to understand what made him bad. In that way I learned what traits to acquire and what faults to avoid. He was teaching me by example and I didn't know I was being taught.

I did not have to come to America to learn the story of George Washington and the cherry tree. My father told me about that famous episode in Birmingham, England. He loved the truth! And for that reason the story appealed to him. He had no patience with a liar and he taught me always to be less afraid to tell the truth than to lie.

As I grew older my father's counsel became broader and deeper. He told me more and more about the ways of men; pointed out their finer virtues and their subtler faults; explained to me why he liked some and disliked others.

Conceit was a trait which he detested. I never heard him boast of anything he had ever done. He had one favorite story, which he told me as soon as he felt I could understand it.

"Don't ever get the notion into your head that the people you work for cannot get along without you," he said. "There was once a very bright young man who made himself valuable to his employer. He was clever, industrious and sharp, and rose quickly to a position of some importance. One day a friend unkindly suggested to this clever young man that he was not being paid in just proportion to his worth. The youth decided this was true, and asked for an increase in salary. This was readily granted. The additional money had been given so willingly that he concluded he must be worth even more, and within a few weeks he approached his employer with another demand. This, too, was met, but the youth remained dissatisfied. The third time he filed a request for more money the firm demurred.

"I know all about your business," said the conceited youth, "and either you'll pay me what I'm really worth or I'll leave. You can't get along without me."

"Oh," replied the president of the company, "that's rather a broad statement! What should we do if you were suddenly to die?"

"Well," stammered the young man, "in that case of course you would *have* to get along."

"Then, in this case," retorted the president, "we'll just consider you as dead."

We laughed together over that conceited man's downfall. My father thought it a splendid joke or pretended to. "It taught him a lesson he sadly needed," he added; and I realize now that the purpose of my father's frequent repetition of that story was to give me a lesson I might some day need. Later he amplified the idea by adding:

"Don't think people can't get along without you, for they can. The thing to do is so to live and act that they won't *want* to get along without you."

My father made no distinctions of dress or class between men. There were but two kinds of men in his catalogue—good and bad. If he thought them bad, he told me why, and urged me never to be like them. I remember one day we were stopped on the street by a wreck of humanity. He was dirty, drunken, ill-smelling, and repulsive to the sight.

"That," said my father, after we had passed on, "is what drink does to a man. Take a good look at him, my boy, and remember him always."

I have heard many temperance lectures since but none so vivid or so lasting as that one.

After we came to America, where Father had elected to start life anew, following the failure of his business venture in England, I continued to make those Sunday-morning walks with him to the place of his employment. He was a bookkeeper for a factory in Detroit, Michigan.

If ever I visited the factory during the weekdays, I was permitted to follow him about the place. I learned from him then that any man, no matter how grimy his work made him nor how soiled his clothing, was worthy and fit for me to associate with if he was honest, straightforward, and clean of speech.

Nor was my father more friendly to one man than to another. I never knew him to flatter a rich man or to scorn a poor man. Once he told me that the way to know men is to know what they are thinking; and that the way to know what men are thinking is to listen patiently to their conversation.

From my father I learned in that way that every honest man who does his work well is a good citizen. I had heard it said that clothes do not make the man; my father taught me to understand that statement. Had I been allowed to judge by appearances I should have lost many a true friend.

We were English until the month of May, 1891. Then we left England to become American. The first legal act that I performed as a man of twenty-one years was to swear allegiance to the Stars and Stripes.

"The United States," Father said to me, "is the greatest country on earth. In no other country are people so happy, so prosperous, and so content. Whatever any man may tell you in the future, be loyal to this Government. Respect its flag and honor its institutions. This is the land of opportunity. I wish I had come here sooner. But you will grow up here, and I want you to be an American citizen. Under this country's flag you can become anything you wish, if you have the strength and the ability and the will to persevere. Here you may live your life unhampered. Remember England kindly as the land of your birth, but stick to and stand by the United States, the land of your opportunity!"

Never in his six brief years of hard struggle—and he encountered the panic of 1892—or of the happiness and peace which came to him as his life was closing, did he once regret his coming here. Not once did he compare the United States unfavorably to England. To him this was the better land. Its interests were his interests, and he entered as far as he could into the support of all things which make for Americanism. From the day we joined him here, the United States was his homeland and his country, which he bade us to love and to serve.

I find that I have but barely touched the account of my indebtedness to my father. I have purposely omitted the items of common need which he furnished, always gladly, however great the personal sacrifice entailed. I have taken for granted the years of my schooling, as I have all the things which called merely for an expenditure of money.

He left us little in the way of worldly wealth; but today, as I run over the pages of my memory and recall the splendor of his service, I find that my debt to him is one which the best I shall ever do, or be, will but partially repay.

For the bigger and finer things of life were his bequests to me.

I owe to him the years of peace and comfort that have been mine.

I have made good friends and true, because my father taught me how lasting friendships are made.

I have found much happiness in life, because he taught me where happiness could be found.

I have traveled not far, but safely, because he taught me wisely.

I have been spared regret and shame and misery and the embarrassment of thoughtless follies by the tact and genius of his counsel; and scarcely a day goes by, even now, that I do not discover, in my heritage from him, some new vein of riches.

                  The End

Chapter 3

Poems about Motherhood and Fatherhood

Little Feet

There is no music quite so sweet
As patter of a baby's feet.
Who never hears along the hall
The sound of tiny feet that fall
Upon the floor so soft and low
As eagerly they come or go,
Has missed, no matter who he be,
Life's most inspiring symphony.

There is a music of the spheres
Too fine to ring in mortal ears,
Yet not more delicate and sweet
Than pattering of baby feet;
Where'er I hear that pit-a-pat
Which falls upon the velvet mat,
Out of my dreamy nap I start
And hear the echo in my heart.

'Tis difficult to put in words
The music of the summer birds,
Yet far more difficult a thing—
A lyric for that pattering;
Here is a music telling me
Of golden joys that are to be;
Unheralded by horns and drums,
To me a regal caller comes.

Now on my couch I lie and hear
A little toddler coming near,
Coming right boldly to my place
To pull my hair and pat my face,
Undaunted by my age or size,
Nor caring that I am not wise—
A visitor devoid of sham
Who loves me just for what I am.

This soft low music tells to me
In just a minute I shall be
Made captive by a thousand charms,
Held fast by chubby little arms,
For there is one upon the way
Who thinks the world was made for play.
Oh, where's the sound that's half so sweet
As pattering of baby feet?

A Boy and His Dad

A boy and his dad on a fishing-trip—
There is a glorious fellowship!
Father and son and the open sky
And the white clouds lazily drifting by,
And the laughing stream as it runs along
With the clicking reel like a martial song,
And the father teaching the youngster gay
How to land a fish in the sportsman's way.

I fancy I hear them talking there
In an open boat, and the speech is fair.
And the boy is learning the ways of men
From the finest man in his youthful ken.
Kings, to the youngster, cannot compare
With the gentle father who's with him there.
And the greatest mind of the human race
Not for one minute could take his place.

Which is happier, man or boy?
The soul of the father is steeped in joy,
For he's finding out, to his heart's delight,
That his son is fit for the future fight.
He is learning the glorious depths of him,
And the thoughts he thinks and his every whim;
And he shall discover, when night comes on,
How close he has grown to his little son.

A boy and his dad on a fishing-trip—
Builders of life's companionship!
Oh, I envy them, as I see them there
Under the sky in the open air,
For out of the old, old long-ago
Come the summer days that I used to know,
When I learned life's truths from my father's lips
As I shared the joy of his fishing-trips.

To the Boy

I have no wish, my little lad,
To climb the towering heights of fame.
I am content to be your dad
And share with you each pleasant game.
I am content to hold your hand
And walk along life's path with you,
And talk of things we understand—
The birds and trees and skies of blue.

Though some may seek the smiles of kings,
For me your laughter's joy enough;
I have no wish to claim the things
Which lure men into pathways rough.
I'm happiest when you and I,
Unmindful of life's bitter cares,
Together watch the clouds drift by,
Or follow boyhood's thoroughfares.

I crave no more of life than this:
Continuance of such a trust;
Your smile, whate'er the morning is,
Until my clay returns to dust.
If but this comradeship may last
Until I end my earthly task—
Your hand and mine by love held fast—
Fame has no charm for which I'd ask.

I would not trade one day with you
To wear the purple robes of power,
Nor drop your hand from mine to do
Some great deed in a selfish hour.
For you have brought me joy serene
And made my soul supremely glad.
In life rewarded I have been;
'Twas all worth while to be your dad.

Baby Feet

Tell me, what is half so sweet
As a baby's tiny feet,
Pink and dainty as can be,
Like a coral from the sea?
Talk of jewels strung in rows,
Gaze upon those little toes,
Fairer than a diadem,
With the mother kissing them!

It is morning and she lies
Uttering her happy cries,
While her little hands reach out
For the feet that fly about.
Then I go to her and blow
Laughter out of every toe;
Hold her high and let her place
Tiny footprints on my face.

Little feet that do not know
Where the winding roadways go,
Little feet that never tire,
Feel the stones or trudge the mire,
Still too pink and still too small
To do anything but crawl,
Thinking all their wanderings fair,
Filled with wonders everywhere.

Little feet, so rich with charm,
May you never come to harm.
As I bend and proudly blow
Laughter out of every toe,
This pray, that God above
Shall protect you with His love,
And shall guide those little feet
Safely down life's broader street.

Story Telling

Most every night when they're in bed,
And both their little prayers have said,
They shout for me to come upstairs
And tell them tales of gypsies bold,
And eagles with the claws that hold
A baby's weight, and fairy sprites
That roam the woods on starry nights.

And I must illustrate these tales,
Must imitate the northern gales
That toss the Indian's canoe,
And show the way he paddles, too.
If in the story comes a bear,
I have to pause and sniff the air
And show the way he climbs the trees
To steal the honey from the bees.

And then I buzz like angry bees
And sting him on his nose and knees
And howl in pain, till mother cries:
"That pair will never shut their eyes,
While all that noise up there you make;
You're simply keeping them awake."
And then they whisper: "Just one more,"
And once again I'm forced to roar.

New stories every night they ask.
And that is not an easy task;
I have to be so many things,
The frog that croaks, the lark that sings,
The cunning fox, the frightened hen;
But just last night they stumped me, when
They wanted me to twist and squirm
And imitate an angle worm.

At last they tumble off to sleep,
And softly from their room I creep
And brush and comb the shock of hair
I tossed about to be a bear.
Then mother says: "Well, I should say
You're just as much a child as they."
But you can bet I'll not resign
That story telling job of mine.

Mother's Job

I'm just the man to make things right,
To mend a sleigh or make a kite,
Or wrestle on the floor and play
Those rough and tumble games, but say!
Just let him get an ache or pain,
And start to whimper and complain,
And from my side he'll quickly flee
To clamber on his mother's knee.

I'm good enough to be his horse
And race with him along the course.
I'm just the friend he wants each time
There is a tree he'd like to climb,
And I'm the pal he's eager for
When we approach a candy store;
But for his mother straight he makes
Whene'er his little stomach aches.

He likes, when he is feeling well,
The kind of stories that I tell,
And I'm his comrade and his chum
And I must march behind his drum.
To me through thick and thin he'll stick,
Unless he happens to be sick.
In which event, with me he's through—
Only his mother then will do.

No Children!

No children in the house to play—
It must be hard to live that way!
I wonder what the people do
When night comes on and the work is through,
With no glad little folks to shout,
No eager feet to race about,
No youthful tongues to chatter on
About the joy that's been and gone?
The house might be a castle fine,
But what a lonely place to dine!

No children in the house at all,
No fingermarks upon the wall,
No corner where the toys are piled—
Sure indication of a child.
No little lips to breathe the prayer
That God shall keep you in His care,
No glad caress and welcome sweet
When night returns you to your street;
No little lips a kiss to give—
Oh, what a lonely way to live!

No children in the house! I fear
We could not stand it half a year.
What would we talk about at night,
Plan for and work with all our might,
Hold common dreams about and find
True union of heart and mind,
If we two had no greater care
Than what we both should eat and wear?
We never knew love's brightest flame
Until the day the baby came.

And now we could not get along
Without their laughter and their song.

Joy is not bottled on a shelf,
It cannot feed upon itself,
And even love, if it shall wear,
Must find its happiness in care;
Dull we'd become of mind and speech
Had we no little ones to teach.
No children in the house to play!
Oh, we could never live that way!

Questions

Would you sell your boy for a stack of gold?
Would you miss that hand that is yours to hold?
Would you take a fortune and never see
The man, in a few brief years, he'll be?
Suppose that his body were racked with pain,
How much would you pay for his health again?

Is there money enough in the world to-day
To buy your boy? Could a monarch pay
You silver and gold in so large a sum
That you'd have him blinded or stricken dumb?
How much would you take, if you had the choice,
Never to hear, in this world, his voice?

How much would you take in exchange for all
The joy that is wrapped in that youngster small?
Are there diamonds enough in the mines of earth
To equal your dreams of that youngster's worth?
Would you give up the hours that he's on your knee
The richest man in the world to be?

You may prate of gold, but your fortune lies,

And you know it well, in your boy's bright eyes.
And there's nothing that money can buy or do
That means so much as that boy to you.
Well, which does the most of your time employ,
The chase for gold—or that splendid boy?

Tied Down

'They tie you down,' a woman said,
Whose cheeks should have been flaming red
With shame to speak of children so.
'When babies come you cannot go
In search of pleasure with your friends,
And all your happy wandering ends.
The things you like you cannot do,
For babies make a slave of you.'

I looked at her and said: "Tis true
That children make a slave of you,
And tie you down with many a knot,
But have you never thought to what
It is of happiness and pride
That little babies have you tied?
Do you not miss the greater joys
That come with little girls and boys?

'They tie you down to laughter rare,
To hours of smiles and hours of care,
To nights of watching and to fears;
Sometimes they tie you down to tears
And then repay you with a smile,
And make your trouble all worth while.
They tie you fast to chubby feet,
And cheeks of pink and kisses sweet.

'They fasten you with cords of love
To God divine, who reigns above.

They tie you, whereso'er you roam,
Unto the little place called home;
And over sea or railroad track
They tug at you to bring you back.
The happiest people in the town
Are those the babies have tied down.

'Oh, go your selfish way and free,
But hampered I would rather be,
Yes rather than a kingly crown
I would be, what you term, tied down;
Tied down to dancing eyes and charms,
Held fast by chubby, dimpled arms,
The fettered slave of girl and boy,
And win from them earth's finest joy.'

Rich

Who has a troop of romping youth
    About his parlor floor,
Who nightly hears a round of cheers,
    When he is at the door,
Who is attacked on every side
    By eager little hands
That reach to tug his grizzled mug,
    The wealth of earth commands.

Who knows the joys of girls and boys,
    His lads and lassies, too,
Who's pounced upon and bounced upon
    When his day's work is through,
Whose trousers know the gentle tug
    Of some glad little tot,
The baby of his crew of love,
    Is wealthier than a lot.

Oh, be he poor and sore distressed
    And weary with the fight,
If with a whoop his healthy troop
    Run, welcoming at night,
And kisses greet him at the end
    Of all his toiling grim,
With what is best in life he's blest
And rich men envy him.

The Spirit of the Home

Dishes to wash and clothes to mend,
    And always another meal to plan,
Never the tasks of a mother end
    And oh, so early her day began!
Floors to sweep and the pies to bake,
    And chairs to dust and the beds to make.

Oh, the home is fair when you come at night
    And the meal is good and the children gay,
And the kettle sings in its glad delight
    And the mother smiles in her gentle way;
So great her love that you seldom see
Or catch a hint of the drudgery.
Home, you say, when the day is done,
    Home to comfort and peace and rest;
Home, where the children romp and run—
    There is the place that you love the best!
Yet what would the home be like if you
Had all of its endless tasks to do?
Would it be home if she were not there,
    Brave and gentle and fond and true?
Could you so fragrant a meal prepare?
    Could you the numberless duties do?
What were the home that you love so much,
Lacking her presence and gracious touch?

She is the spirit of all that's fair;
    She is the home that you think you build;
She is the beauty you dream of there;
    She is the laughter with which it's filled—
She, with her love and her gentle smile,
Is all that maketh the home worth while.

Home and the Office

Home is the place where the laughter should ring,
    And man should be found at his best.
Let the cares of the day be as great as they may,
    The night has been fashioned for rest.
So leave at the door when the toiling is o'er
    All the burdens of worktime behind,
And just be a dad to your girl or your lad—
    A dad of the rollicking kind.

The office is made for the tasks you must face;
    It is built for the work you must do;
You may sit there and sigh as your cares pile up high,
    And no one may criticize you;
You may worry and fret as you think of your debt,
    You may grumble when plans go astray,
But when it comes night, and you shut your desk tight,
    Don't carry the burdens away.

Keep daytime for toil and the nighttime for play,
    Work as hard as you choose in the town,
But when the day ends, and the darkness descends,
    Just forget that you're wearing a frown—
Go home with a smile! Oh, you'll find it worth while;
    Go home light of heart and of mind;

Go home and be glad that you're loved as a dad,
    A dad of the fun-loving kind.

When Pa Comes Home

When Pa comes home, I'm at the door,
An' then he grabs me off the floor
An' throws me up an' catches me
When I come down, an' then, says he:
'Well, how'd you get along to-day?
An' were you good, an' did you play,
An' keep right out of mamma's way?
An' how'd you get that awful bump
Above your eye? My, what a lump!
An' who spilled jelly on your shirt?
An' where'd you ever find the dirt
That's on your hands? And my! Oh, my!
I guess those eyes have had a cry,
They look so red. What was it, pray?
What has been happening here to-day?'

An' then he drops his coat an' hat
Upon a chair, an' says: 'What's that?
Who knocked that engine on its back
An' stepped upon that piece of track?"
An' then he takes me on his knee
An' says: 'What's this that now I see?
Whatever can the matter be?
Who strewed those toys upon the floor,
An' left those things behind the door?
Who upset all those parlor chairs
An' threw those blocks upon the stairs?
I guess a cyclone called to-day
While I was workin' far away.
Who was it worried mamma so?
It can't be anyone I know.'

An' then I laugh an' say: 'It's me!
Me did most ever'thing you see.
Me got this bump the time me tripped.
An' here is where the jelly slipped
Right off my bread upon my shirt,
An' when me tumbled down it hurt.
That's how me got all over dirt.
Me threw those building blocks downstairs,
An' me upset the parlor chairs,
Coz when you're playin' train you've got
To move things 'round an awful lot.'
An' then my Pa he kisses me
An' bounces me upon his knee
An' says: 'Well, well, my little lad,
What glorious fun you must have had!'

Daddies

I would rather be the daddy
Of a romping, roguish crew,
Of a bright-eyed chubby laddie
And a little girl or two,
Than the monarch of a nation
In his high and lofty seat
Taking empty adoration
From the subjects at his feet.

I would rather own their kisses
As at night to me they run,
Than to be the king who misses
All the simpler forms of fun.
When his dreary day is ending
He is dismally alone,
But when my sun is descending

There are joys for me to own.
He may ride to horns and drumming;
I must walk a quiet street,
But when once they see me coming
Then on joyous, flying feet
They come racing to me madly
And I catch them with a swing
And I say it proudly, gladly,
That I'm happier than a king.

You may talk of lofty places,
You may boast of pomp and power,
Men may turn their eager faces
To the glory of an hour,
But give me the humble station
With its joys that long survive,
For the daddies of the nation
Are the happiest men alive.

She Mothered Five

She mothered five!
Night after night she watched a little bed,
Night after night she cooled a fevered head,
Day after day she guarded little feet,
Taught little minds the dangers of the street,
Taught little lips to utter simple prayers,
Whispered of strength that some day would be theirs,
And trained them all to use it as they should.
She gave her babies to the nation's good.
She mothered five!
She gave her beauty—from her cheeks let fade
Their rose-blush beauty—to her mother trade.
She saw the wrinkles furrowing her brow,
Yet smiling said: "My boy grows stronger now."
When pleasures called she turned away and said:

"I dare not leave my babies to be fed
By strangers' hands; besides they are too small;
I must be near to hear them when they call."

She mothered five!
Night after night they sat about her knee
And heard her tell of what some day would be.
From her they learned that in the world outside
Are cruelty and vice and selfishness and pride;
From her they learned the wrongs they ought to shun,
What things to love, what work must still be done.
She led them through the labyrinth of youth
And brought five men and women up to truth.

She mothered five!
Her name may be unknown save to the few;
Of her the outside world but little knew;
But somewhere five are treading virtue's ways,
Serving the world and brightening its days;
Somewhere are five, who, tempted, stand upright,
Who cling to honor, keep her memory bright;
Somewhere this mother toils and is alive
No more as one, but in the breasts of five.

Chapter 4

Edgar's First Three Books of Poetry

Shortly after the Guest family arrived in Detroit from England, Edgar's father lost the job that was to provide for his large family. At eleven years of age, Edgar began working after school and on weekends to help his family. His sunny disposition and warm personality opened doors of opportunity for him, and he advanced from job to job as he grew. He began as a boy who watered horses; then worked at first one drugstore, and then another—at each job taking on more and more responsibility. Then one important day in 1895, he was offered a job at the Detroit Free Press, which he accepted.

Edgar joyfully stayed on payroll of the *Detroit* for the rest of his life but also pursued many other opportunities. Sadly, Edgar never finished high school. After his father's death, Edgar needed to work to help provide for his mother and family.

At the *Detroit Free Press*, he began as a copy boy in the accounting and business department. Two years later, he worked up the courage to ask for a position in the editorial department.

He started as a cub reporter, then became a marine reporter, and then a police reporter—which is where he really began to build a name for himself. He also began to work for the exchange editor. It was during this time that he became familiar with the common practice of publishing poetry in the daily newspapers.

One of his jobs was to find good poems from other newspapers that could be printed with his press. This work inspired him to try writing his own poems. One day he slipped a poem under the door of the Sunday editor, Arthur Mosely. It was printed on December 11, 1898.

Edgar began writing a daily column titled "Breakfast Table Chat" in 1904. Edgar established the practice of starting each day's column with an original verse. He would carry on this practice of a verse a day for decades, never missing a deadline.

Edgar's first book, entitled *Home Rhymes*, was published in 1910. Because no book publisher had recognized Edgar's work, the book was self-published. Edgar's brother Harry was a printer, and the two brothers partnered on the book.

After buying a case of type, they set it up in the attic. In the evenings, they worked laboriously to set up eight pages of type. They then lugged the type to a print shop, printed the pages, lugged the type back home, broke it up, and started on the next pages. The result was 800 copies of a thin green-covered book.

The next book, *Just Glad Things*, was also self-published by the brothers. They originally printed 1,500 copies of this book.

A couple of years later, the brothers self-published a third book, *Breakfast Table Chat*, and printed 3,500 copies.

Edgar eventually found a publisher for later books, and he authored over 20 volumes of poetry. His fourth volume of poetry, titled *Heap o' Living,* was published in 1916 and sold over one million copies alone.

As you read the following poems from his first three self-published books, ask yourself why you think the poems were received so well by the American people.

The Painter

When my hair is thin and silvered, an' my time of toil is through,
When I've many years behind me, an' ahead of me a few,
I shall want to sit, I reckon, sort of dreamin' in the sun,
An' recall the roads I've traveled an' the many things I've done,
An' I hope there'll be no picture that I'll hate to look upon
When the time to paint it better or to wipe it out is gone.

I hope there'll be no vision of a hasty word I've said,
That has left a trail of sorrow, like a whip welt, sore an' red,
An' I hope my old-age dreamin' will bring back no bitter scene
Of a time when I was selfish an' a time when I was mean;
When I'm gettin' old an' feeble, an' I'm far along life's way
I don't want to sit regrettin' any by-gone yesterday.

I'll admit the children boss me, I'll admit I often smile
When I ought to frown upon 'em, but for such a little while
They are naughty, romping youngsters, that I have no heart to scold,
An' I know if I should whip 'em I'd regret it when I'm old.
Age to me would be a torment an' a ghost-infested night,
If I'd ever hurt a baby, an' I could not make it right.

I am painting now the pictures that I'll some day want to see,

I am filling in a canvas that will come back soon to me.

An' though nothing great is on it, an' though nothing there is fine,

I shall want to look it over when I'm old an' call it mine.

An' I do not dare to leave it, while the paint is warm an' wet,

With a single thing upon it that I'll later on regret.

The Man I'm For

I'm for the happy man every time,
The man who smiles as he goes his way,
Whether he's up or whether he's down,
I'm for the man with a grin, I say.
I'm for the man who can bear his woes
With never a grumbling word or frown,
Who, smiling, gathers the rue or rose—
There is the man that you can't keep down.

I'm for the cheerful man, heart and soul!
His is the hand that I like to grasp;
Who tunes his voice in a merry key,
Not files it down to a bitter rasp.
I'm for the man who can take the cards
Just as they're dealt by the hand of fate,
And, good or bad, play an honest game
With a lifted chin and a smile that's great.

Troubles

Troubles? Sure I've lots of them,
Got 'em heaped up by the score,
Got 'em baled and bundled up,
Got 'em hid behind the door.
Got 'em young and got 'em old,
Got 'em big and little, too.
Don't care to discuss 'em now,
Rather tell my joys to you.

Got the finest home there is,
Got the finest pair o' boys,
An' the sweetest little girl,

Reg'lar livin', breathin' joys.
Got the finest wife in town,
Got a little garden, too.
Troubles? Sure I've got 'em, but
Rather tell my joys to you.

Got a bunch of friends I love,
Friends I know are staunch and true;
Visit 'em, they visit me,
Jus' the way good friends should do;
Got my health, an' got a job,
That's enough to see me through.
Troubles? Sure I've got 'em, but
Rather tell my joys to you.

Money

I'd hate to think so much of gold
That I would sell myself to gain it,
I'd hate the sound of metal cold
If I must shamefully attain it.
I'd hate to be so much a slave
To minted silver, gold, and copper,
That I'd forget in moments grave
To do the decent thing and proper.

I'd like to live a life of ease
And tread a pathway always sunny,
But I'd not worship on my knees
The golden idol known as Money.
A man of wealth I'd like to be,
But I would rather dig in ditches
Than ever have it said of me,
I'd sold myself for riches.

Now and Then

Why not think a decent thought,
Now and then?
Why not ponder, as you ought,
Now and then?
Get your mind out of the mire,
To the higher things aspire,
Claim a loftier desire,
Now and then.

Think of something else than gold,
Now and then!
Think of things not bought and sold,
Now and then;
Turn from sordid deeds and mean,
In your acts your thoughts are seen,
Think of something sweet and clean,
Now and then.

Think of good instead of bad,
Now and then;
Of the bright things, not the sad,
Now and then;
If you think the way you should,
As you could think if you would,
You would do a lot of good,
Now and then.

I'll Never Be Rich

I'll never be rich.
I'm too fond of the joy
Of a certain small girl
And a certain small boy;
And the nights full of fun
And the days full of play,
And the romp and the run
At the end of the day.

I'll never be rich.
I'm too eager to share
In the joys that are near,
Too unwilling to care
For the thing we call gold,
That I'll fill every day

Full of strife for the stuff,
And not rest by the way.

I'll never be rich.
There are too many charms
That I now can possess
When I stretch out my arms;
There are too many joys
That already I hold
That I cannot give up
Just to wallow in gold.

Chapter 5

Home

Edgar had been married to Nellie Crossman for four years when his first book of poetry was published. Edgar was known to all his friends as Eddie, but Nellie always addressed him by his full name, Edgar. From Edgar's poetry we get glimpses into the type of woman Nellie was: hard-working, patient, supportive, cheerful, and nurturing.

Here we read the dedication to one of his books:

"All That Matters"
Is Dedicated
To My Wife
Who Is
All To Me

The following two poems by Edgar give deep insight into the couple's loving relationship.

Wife o' Mine

Wife o' Mine, day after day
Cheering me along the way;
Patient, tender, smiling, true,
Always ready to renew
Faltering courage and to share
All the day may bring of care;
Dreaming dreams wherein you see
Brighter years that are to be;
Calling paltry pleasures fine—
That's you always, Wife o' Mine.

Wife o' Mine, we've shed some tears
With the passing of the years,
Mourned beside our lovely dead;
But somehow you've always said
You and I could bear the blow
Knowing God had willed it so;
And you've smiled to show to me
Just how brave you meant to be,
Smiled to keep my faith in line—
That's you, always, Wife o' Mine.

Wife o' Mine, long years ago
Once I promised you would know
Luxuries and costly things,
Gowns of silk and jeweled rings,
And you laughed as though you knew
Dreams like that could not come true;
Now perhaps they never will,

But I see you laughing still,
Welcoming me with eyes that shine—
That's you always, Wife o' Mine.

A Cup of Tea

Nellie made a cup of tea,
Made and poured it out for me,
And above the steaming brew
Smiled and asked me: "One or two?"
Saucily she tossed her head,
"Make it sweet for me," I said.

Two sweet lumps of sugar fell
Into that small china well,
But I knew the while I drained
Every drop the cup contained,
More than sugar in the tea
Made the beverage sweet for me.

This to her I tried to say
In that golden yesterday—
Life is like a cup of tea
Which Time poureth endlessly,
Brewed by trial's constant heat,
Needing love to make it sweet.

Then I caught her looking up,
And I held my dainty cup
Out to her and bravely said:
"Here is all that lies ahead,
Here is all my life to be—
Will you make it sweet for me?"

That was years ago, and now

There is silver in her brow;
We have sorrowed, we have smiled,
We've been hurt and reconciled—
But whatever had to be,
She has made it sweet for me.

Edgar and Nellie's home lives were not without trial. The following short book by Edgar Guest, *Making the House a Home*, shows how this devoted couple experienced the full gamut of human experience and came out better for it in the end.

Making the House a Home

We have been building a home for the last fifteen years, but it begins to look now as though it will not be finished for many years to come. This is not because the contractors are slow, or the materials scarce, or because we keep changing our minds. Rather it is because it takes years to build a home, whereas a house can be builded in a few months.

Mother and I started this home-building job on June 28th, 1906. I was twenty-five years of age; and she—well, it is sufficient for the purposes of this record to say that she was a few years younger. I was just closing my career as police reporter for the Detroit "Free Press," when we were married. Up to a few months before our wedding, my hours had been from three o'clock, in the afternoon, until three o'clock in the morning, every day of the week except Friday. Those are not fit hours for a married man—especially a young married man. So it was fortunate for me that my managing editor thought I might have possibilities as a special writer, and relieved me from night duty.

It was then we began to plan the home we should build. It was to be a hall of contentment and the abiding place of joy and beauty. And it was all going to be done on the splendid salary of twenty-eight dollars a week. That sum doesn't sound like much now, but to us, in January, 1906, it was independence. The foundation of our first home was something less than five hundred dollars, out of which was also to come the extravagance of a two-weeks' honeymoon trip.

Fortunately for all of us, life does not break its sad news in advance. Dreams are free, and in their flights of fancy young folks may be as extravagant as they wish. There may be breakers ahead, and trials, days of discouragement and despair, but life tells us nothing of them to spoil our dreaming.

We knew the sort of home we wanted, but we were willing to begin humbly. This was not because we were averse to starting at the top. Both Mother and I had then, and have now, a fondness for the best things of life. We should have liked a grand piano, and a self-making ice box, and a servant, and an automobile right off! But less than five hundred dollars capital and twenty-eight dollars a week salary do not provide those things.

What we could have would be a comfortable flat, and some nice furniture. We'd pay cash for all we could, and buy the remainder of the necessary things on time. We had found a wonderful, brand-new flat which we could rent for twenty-five dollars a month. It had hardwood floors, steam heat, two big bedrooms, a fine living room with a gas grate, a hot-water heater for the bath, and everything modern and convenient. Today the landlord would ask ninety dollars a month for that place and tell you he was losing money at that.

With the rent paid, we should have eighty-seven dollars a month left to live on. The grocery bill, at that time, would not run more than twenty dollars a month; telephone, gas, and electric light would not exceed ten dollars a month; the milkman and the paper boy would take but little, and in winter time a ton of coal per month would be sufficient. Oh, we should have plenty of money, and could easily afford to pledge twenty dollars a month to pay for necessary furniture.

It will be noticed that into our dreaming came no physician, no dentist, no expenses bobbing up from unexpected sources. Not a single bill collector called at the front door of our dream castle to ask for money which we did not have.

If older and wiser heads suggested the possibility of danger, we produced our plans on paper, and asked them from whence could trouble come? To-day we understand the depth of the kindly smile which our protests always evoked. They were letting the dreamers dream.

At last the furniture was bought on the installment plan and the new flat was being put in order. It called for a few more pieces of furniture than we had figured on, and the debt, in consequence, was greater; but that meant merely a few months more to make payments.

It was fine furniture, too! Of course it has long since ceased to serve us; but never in this world shall that dining set be duplicated! For perfection of finish and loveliness of design, that first oak dining table will linger in our memories for life. The one we now have cost more than all the money we spent for all the furniture with which we began housekeeping; and yet, figuring according to the joy it has brought to us, it is poor in comparison.

And so it was, too, with the mahogany settee, upholstered in green plush, and the beveled glass dresser, and the living-room chairs. We used to make evening trips over to that flat merely for the joy of admiring these things—our things; the first we had ever possessed.

Then came the night of June 27th. We had both looked forward to that wonderful honeymoon trip up the lakes to Mackinac Island, and tomorrow we were to start. But right then I am sure that both Mother and I wished we might call it off. It seemed so foolish to go away from such a beautiful flat and such lovely furniture.

The honeymoon trip lasted two weeks; and one day, at Mackinac Island, I found Mother in tears.

"What the matter?" I asked.

"I want to go home!" she said. "I know I am silly and foolish, but I want to get back to our own house and our own furniture, and arrange our wedding presents, and hang the curtains, and put that set of Haviland china in the cabinet!"

So back we came to begin our home-building in earnest.

The rent and the furniture installments came due regularly, just as we had expected. So did the gas and electric light and telephone bills. But, somehow or other, our dream figures and the actual realities did not balance. There never was a month when there was as much left of our eighty-seven dollars as we had figured there should have been.

For one thing, I was taken ill. That brought the doctor into the house; and since then we have always had him to reckon with and to settle with.

Then there was an insurance policy to keep up. In our dream days, the possibility of my dying sometime had never entered our heads; but now it was an awful reality. And that quarterly premium developed a distressing habit of falling due at the most inopportune times. Just when we thought we should have at least twenty dollars for ourselves, in would come the little yellow slip informing us that the thirty days' grace expired on the fifth.

But the home-of-our-own was still in our dreams. We were happy, but we were going to be still happier. If ever we could get rid of those furniture installments we could start saving for the kind of home we wanted.

Then, one evening, Mother whispered the happiest message a wife ever tells a husband. We were no longer to live merely for ourselves; there was to be another soon, who should bind us closer together and fill our lives with gladness.

But—and many a night we sat for hours and

planned and talked and wondered—how were we to meet the expense? There was nothing in the savings bank, and much was needed there. Mother had cherished for years her ideas for her baby's outfit. They would cost money; and I would be no miserly father, either! My child should have the best of everything, somehow. It was up to me to get it, somehow, to. . . . If only that furniture were paid for!

Then a curious event occurred. I owed little bills amounting to about twenty-one dollars. This sum included the gas, electric light, and telephone bills, on which an added sum was charged if unpaid before the tenth of the month. I had no money to meet them. I was worried and discouraged. To borrow that sum would have been easy, but to pay it back would have been difficult.

That very morning, into the office came the press agent of a local theatre, accompanied by Mr. Henry Dixey, the well-known actor. Mr. Dixey wanted two lyrics for songs. He had the ideas which he wished expressed in rhyme, and wondered whether or not I would attempt them. I promised him that I would, and on the spot he handed me twenty-five dollars in cash to bind the bargain. If those songs proved successful I should have more.

The way out had been provided! From Mr. Dixey's point of view, those songs were not a success; but from mine they were, for they bridged me over a chasm I had thought I could not leap. I never heard from that pair of songs afterward; but neither Mother nor I will ever forget the day they were written.

It meant more than the mere paying of bills, too. It taught us to have faith—faith in ourselves and faith in the future. There is always a way out of the difficulties. Even though we cannot see or guess what that way is to be, it will be provided. Since then we have gone together through many dark days and cruel hurts and bitter disappointments, but always to come out stronger for the test.

The next few months were devoted to preparations for the baby, and our financial reckonings had to be readjusted. I had to find ways of making a little more money. I was not after much money, but I must have more. All I had to sell was what I could write. Where was a quick market for a poor newspaper man's wares?

My experience with Mr. Dixey turned me to the vaudeville stage. I could write playlets, I thought. So while Mother was busy sewing at nights I devoted myself to writing. And at last the first sketch was finished. At the Temple Theatre that week was the popular character actor, William H. Thompson. To him I showed the manuscript of the sketch, which was called "The Matchmaker." Mr. Thompson took it on Tuesday; and on Friday he sent word that he wished to see me. Into his dressing-room I went, almost afraid to face him.

"It's a bully little sketch," said he, as I sat on his trunk, "and I'd like to buy it from you. I can't pay as much as I should like; but if you care to let me have it I'll give you two hundred and fifty dollars—one hundred and fifty dollars now, and the remaining hundred next week."

I tried to appear indifferent, but the heart of me was almost bursting with excitement. It meant that the furniture bill was as good as paid! And there would be money in the bank for the first time since we were married! The deal was made, and I left the theatre with the largest sum of money I had ever made all at once. Later someone said to me that I was foolish to sell that sketch outright for so little money.

"Foolish!" said I. "That two hundred and fifty dollars looked bigger to me than the promise of a thousand some day in the future!"

Once more the way out had been provided.

And then came the baby—a glorious little girl [Florence, nicknamed Jessie]—and the home had begun to be worth-while. There was a new charm to the walls and halls. The oak table and the green plush settee took on a new glory.

I was the usual proud father, with added variations of my own. One of my pet illusions was that none, save Mother and me, was to be trusted to hold our little one. When others would take her, I stood guard to catch her if in some careless moment they should let her fall.

As she grew older, my collars became finger-marked where her little hands had touched them. We had pictures on our walls, of course, and trinkets on the mantelpiece, and a large glass mirror which had been one of our wedding gifts. These things had become commonplace to us—until the baby began to notice them! Night after night, I would take her in my arms and show her the sheep in one of the pictures, and talk to her about them, and she would coo delightedly. The trinkets on the mantelpiece became dearer to us because she loved to handle them. The home was being sanctified by her presence. We had come into a new realm of happiness.

But a home cannot be builded always on happiness. We were to learn that through bitter experience. We had seen white crepe on other doors, without ever thinking that some day it might flutter on our own. We had witnessed sorrow, but had never suffered it. Our home had welcomed many a gay and smiling visitor; but there was a grim and sinister one to come, against whom no door can be barred.

After thirteen months of perfect happiness, its planning and dreaming, the baby was taken from us.

The blow fell without warning. I left home that morning, with Mother and the baby waving their usual farewells to me from the window. Early that afternoon, contrary to my usual custom, I decided to go home in advance of my regular time. I had no reason for doing this, aside from a strange unwillingness to continue at work. I recalled later that I cleaned up my desk and put away a number of things, as though I were going away for some time. I never before had done that, and nothing had occurred which might make me think I should not be back at my desk as usual.

When I reached home the baby was suffering from a slight fever, and Mother already had called the doctor in. He diagnosed it as only a slight disturbance.

During dinner, I thought baby's breathing was not as regular as it should be, and I summoned the doctor immediately. Her condition grew rapidly worse, and a second physician was called; but it was not in human skill to save her. At eleven o'clock that night she was taken from us.

It is needless to dwell here upon the agony of that first dark time through which we passed. That such a blow could leave loveliness in its path, and add a touch of beauty to our dwelling place, seemed unbelievable at the time. Yet to-day our first baby still lives with us, as wonderful as she was in those glad thirteen months. She has not grown older, as have we, but smiles that same sweet baby smile of hers upon us as of old. We can talk of her now bravely and proudly; and we have come to understand that it was a privilege to have had her, even for those brief thirteen months.

To have joys in common is the dream of man and wife. We had supposed that love was based on mutual happiness. And Mother and I had been happy together; we had been walking arm in arm under blue skies, and we knew how much we meant to each other. But just how much we needed each other neither of us really knew—until we had to share a common sorrow.

To be partners in a sacred memory is a divine

bond. To be partners in a little mound, in one of God's silent gardens, is the closest relationship which man and woman can know on this earth. Our lives had been happy before; now they had been made beautiful.

So it was with the home. It began to mean more to us, as we began each to mean more to the other. The bedroom in which our baby fell asleep seemed glorified. Of course there were the lonely days and weeks and months when everything we touched or saw brought back the memory of her. I came home many an evening to find on Mother's face the mark of tears; and I knew she had been living over by herself the sorrow of it all.

I learned how much braver the woman has to be than the man. I could go into town, where there was the contagion of good cheer; and where my work absorbed my thoughts and helped to shut out grief. But not so with Mother! She must live day by day and hour by hour amid the scenes of her anguish. No matter where she turned, something reminded her of the joy we had known and lost. Even the striking clock called back to her mind the hour when something should have been done for the baby.

"I must have another little girl," she sobbed night after night. "I must have another little girl!"

And once more the way out was provided. We heard of a little girl who was to be put out for adoption; she was of good but unfortunate parents. We proposed to adopt her.

I have heard many arguments against adopting children, but I have never heard a good one. Even the infant doomed to die could enrich, if only for a few weeks, the lives of a childless couple, and they would be happier for the rest of their days in the knowledge that they had tried to do something worthy in this world and had made comfortable the brief life of a little one.

"What if the child should turn out wrong?" I hear often from the lips of men and women.

"What of that?" I reply. "You can at least be happy in the thought that you have tried to do something for another."

To childless couples everywhere I would say with all the force I can employ, adopt a baby! If you would make glorious the home you are building; if you would fill its rooms with laughter and contentment; if you would make your house more than a place in which to eat and sleep; if you would fill it with happy memories and come yourselves into a closer and more perfect union, adopt a baby! Then, in a year or two, adopt another. He who spends money on a little child is investing it to real purpose; and the dividends it pays in pride and happiness and contentment are beyond computation.

Marjorie came to us when she was three years old. She bubbled over with mirth and laughter and soothed the ache in our hearts. She filled the little niches and corners of our lives with her sweetness, and became not only ours in name, but ours also in love and its actualities.

There were those who suggested that we were too young to adopt a child. They told us that the other children would undoubtedly be sent to us as time went on. I have neither the space here nor the inclination to list the imaginary difficulties outlined to us as the possibilities of adoption.

But Mother and I talked it all over one evening. And we decided that we needed Marjorie, and Marjorie needed us. As to the financial side of the question, I smiled.

"I never heard of anyone going to the poorhouse, or into bankruptcy," I said, "because of the money spent on a child. I fancy I can pay the bills."

That settled it. The next evening when I came home, down the stairway leading to our flat came the cry, "Hello, Daddy!" from one of the sweetest little faces I have ever seen. And from that day, until God needed her more and called her home, that "Hello, Daddy" greeted me and made every care worth while.

The little home had begun to grow in beauty once more. That first shopping tour for Marjorie stands out as an epoch in our lives. I am not of the right sex to describe it. Marjorie came to us with only such clothing as a poor mother could provide. She must be outfitted anew from head to toe, and she was. The next evening, when she greeted me, she was the proud possessor of more lovely things than she had ever known before. But, beautiful as the little face appeared to me then, more beautiful was the look in Mother's face. There had come into her eyes a look of happiness which had been absent for many months. I learned then, and I state it now as a positive fact, that a woman's greatest happiness comes from dressing a little girl. Mothers may like pretty clothes for themselves; but to put pretty things on a little girl is an infinitely greater pleasure. More than once Mother went down-town for something for herself— only to return without it, but with something for Marjorie!

We pledged to ourselves at the very beginning that we would make Marjorie ours; not only to ourselves but to others. Our friends were asked never to refer in her presence to the fact that she was adopted. As far as we were concerned it was dismissed from our minds. She was three years old when she was born to us, and from then on we were her father and her mother. To many who knew her and loved her, this article will be the first intimation they ever have received that Marjorie was not our own flesh and blood. It was her pride and boast that she was like her mother, but had her father's eyes. Both her mother and I have smiled hundreds of times, as people meeting her for the first time would say, "Anyone would know she belonged to you. She looks exactly like you!"

Marjorie made a difference in our way of living. A second-story flat, comfortable though it was, was not a good place to bring up a little girl. More than ever, we needed a home of our own. But to need and to provide are two different propositions. We needed a back yard; but back yards are expensive; and though newspapermen may make good husbands they seldom make "good money."

One evening Mother announced to me that she had seen the house we ought to have. It had just been completed, had everything in it her heart had wished for, and could be bought for forty-two hundred dollars. The price was just forty-two hundred dollars more than I had!

All I did have was the wish to own a home of my own. But four years of our married life had gone, and I was no nearer the first payment on a house than when we began as man and wife. However, I investigated and found that I could get this particular house by paying five hundred dollars down and agreeing to pay thirty-five a month on the balance. I could swing thirty-five a month, but the five hundred was a high barrier.

Then I made my first wise business move. I went to Julius Haass, president of the Wayne County and Home Savings Bank, who always had been my friend, and explained to him my difficulties. He loaned me that five hundred dollars for the first payment—I to pay it back twenty-five dollars monthly—and the house was ours.

We had become land owners overnight. My income had increased, of course; but so had my liabilities. The first few years of that new house taxed our ingenuity more than once. We spent now and then, not money which we had, but money which we were going to get; but it was buying happiness. If ever a couple have found real happiness in this world we found it under the roof of that Leicester Court home.

There nearly all that has brought joy and peace

and contentment into our lives was born to us. It was from there I began to progress; it was there my publishers found me; and it was there little Bud was born to us. We are out of it now. We left it for a big reason; but we drive by it often just to see it; for it is still ours in the precious memory of the years we spent within its walls.

Still, in the beginning, it was just a house! It had no associations and no history. It had been built to sell. The people who paid for its construction saw in its growing walls and rooftree only the few hundred dollars they hoped to gain. It was left to us to change that house into a home. It sounds preachy, I know, to say that all buildings depend for their real beauty upon the spirit of the people who inhabit them. But it is true.

As the weeks and months slipped by, the new house began to soften and mellow under Mother's gentle touches. The living-room assumed an air of comfort; my books now had a real corner of their own; the guest-chamber—or, rather, the little spare-room—already had entertained its transient tenants; and as our friends came and went the walls caught something from them all, to remind us of their presence.

I took to gardening. The grounds were small, but they were large enough to teach me the joy of an intimate friendship with growing things. To-day, in my somewhat larger garden, I have more than one hundred and fifty rosebushes, and twenty or thirty peony clumps, and I know their names and their habits. The garden has become a part of the home. It is not yet the garden I dream of, nor even the garden which I think it will be next year; but it is the place where play divides the ground with beauty. What Bud doesn't require for a baseball diamond the roses possess.

Early one morning in July, Bud came to us. Immediately, the character of that front bedroom was changed. It was no longer just "our bedroom;"

it was "the room where Bud was born." Of all the rooms in all the houses of all the world, there is none so gloriously treasured in the memories of man and woman as those wherein their children have come to birth.

I have had many fine things happen to me: Friends have borne me high on kindly shoulders; out of the depths of their generous hearts they have given me honors which I have not deserved; I have more than once come home proud in the possession of some new joy, or of some task accomplished; but I have never known, and never shall know, a thrill of happiness to equal that which followed good old Doctor Gordon's brief announcement: "It's a Boy!"

"It's a Boy!" All that day and the next I fairly shouted it to friends and strangers. To Marjorie's sweetness, and to the radiant loveliness of the little baby which was ours for so brief a time, had been added the strength and roguishness of a boy.

The next five years saw the walls of our home change in character. Finger marks and hammer marks began to appear. When Bud had reached the stage where he could walk, calamity began to follow in his trail. Once he tugged at a table cover and the open bottle of ink fell upon the rug. There was a great splotch of ink forever to be visible to all who entered that living-room! Yet even that black stain became in time a part of us. We grew even to boast of it. We pointed it out to new acquaintances as the place where Bud spilled the ink. It was an evidence of his health and his natural tendencies. It proved to all the world that in Bud we had a real boy; an honest-to-goodness boy who could spill ink—and would, if you didn't keep a close watch on him.

Then came the toy period of our development. The once tidy house became a place where angels would have feared to tread in the dark. Building blocks and trains of cars and fire engines and a rocking horse were everywhere, to trip the feet of the unwary. Mother scolded about it, at times; and

I fear I myself have muttered harsh things when, late at night, I have entered the house only to stumble against the tin sides of an express wagon.

But I have come to see that toys in a house are its real adornments. There is no pleasanter sight within the front door of any man's castle than the strewn and disordered evidences that children there abide. The house seems unfurnished without them.

This chaos still exists in our house to-day. Mother says I encourage it. Perhaps I do. I know that I dread the coming day when the home shall become neat and orderly and silent and precise. What is more, I live in horror of the day when I shall have to sit down to a meal and not send a certain little fellow away from the table to wash his hands. That has become a part of the ceremonial of my life. When the evening comes that he will appear for dinner, clean and immaculate, his shirt buttoned properly and his hair nicely brushed, perhaps Mother will be proud of him; but as for me, there will be a lump in my throat—for I shall know that he has grown up.

Financially, we were progressing. We had a little more "to do with," as Mother expressed it; but sorrow and grief and anxiety were not through with us.

We were not to be one hundred per cent happy. No one ever is. Marjorie was stricken with typhoid fever, and for fourteen weeks we fought that battle; saw her sink almost into the very arms of death; and watched her pale and wasted body day by day, until at last the fever broke and she was spared to us.

Another bedroom assumed a new meaning to us both. We knew it as it was in the dark hours of night; we saw the morning sun break through its windows. It was the first room I visited in the morning and the last I went to every night. Coming home, I never stopped in hall or living-room, but hurried straight to her. All there was in that home then was Marjorie's room! We lived our lives within it. And gradually, her strength returned and we were happy again.

But only for a brief time. . . . Early the following summer I was called home by Doctor Johnson. When I reached there, he met me at the front door, smiling as though to reassure me.

"You and Bud are going to get out," said he. "Marjorie has scarlet fever."

Bud had already been sent to his aunt Florence's. I was to gather what clothing I should need for six weeks and depart.

If I had been fond of that home before, I grew fonder of it as the days went by. I think I never knew how much I valued it until I was shut out from it. I could see Mother and Marjorie through the window, but I was not to enter. And I grew hungry for a sight of the walls with their finger marks, and of the ink spot on the rug. We had been six years in the building of that home. Somehow, a part of us had been woven into every nook and corner of it.

But Marjorie was not thriving. Her cheeks were pale and slightly flushed. The removal of tonsils didn't help. Followed a visit to my dentist. Perhaps a tooth was spreading poison through her system. He looked at her, and after a few minutes took me alone into his private office.

"I'm sorry, Eddie," he said. "I am afraid it isn't teeth. You have a long, hard fight to make—if it is what I think it is."

Tuberculosis had entered our home. It had come by way of typhoid and scarlet fevers. The specialist confirmed Doctor Oakman's suspicions, and our battle began. The little home could serve us no longer. It was not the place for such a fight for life as we were to make. Marjorie must have a wide-open sleeping porch; and the house lacked that, nor could one be built upon it.

And so we found our present home. It was for sale at a price I thought then I should never be able to pay. We could have it by making a down payment of seventy-five hundred dollars, the balance to be covered by a mortgage. But I neither had that much, nor owned securities for even a small fraction of it.

But I did have a friend: a rich, but generous friend! I told him what I wanted; and he seemed more grieved at my burden than concerned with my request. He talked only of Marjorie and her chances; he put his arm about my shoulders, and I knew he was with me.

"What do you need?" he asked.

"Seventy-five hundred dollars in cash."

He smiled.

"Have a lawyer examine the abstract to the property, and if it is all right come back to me."

In two days I was back. The title to the house was clear. He smiled again, and handed me his check for the amount, with not a scratch of the paper between us.

I suggested something of that sort to him.

"The important thing is to get the house," he said. "When that is done and you have the deed to it and the papers all fixed up, you come back and we'll fix up our little matter." And that is how it was done.

So into our present home we moved. We had a bigger and a better and a costlier dwelling place. We were climbing upward. But we were also beginning once more with just a house. Just a house—but founded on a mighty purpose! It was to become home to us, even more dearly loved than the one we were leaving.

For four years it has grown in our affections. Hope has been ours. We have lived and laughed and sung and progressed. . . . But we have also wept and grieved.

Twice the doctor had said we were to conquer. Then came last spring and the end of hope. Week after week, Marjorie saw the sunbeams filter through the windows of her open porch; near by, a pair of robins built their nest; she watched them and knew them and named them. We planned great things together and great journeys we should make. That they were not to be she never knew. . . . And then she fell asleep—

Her little life had fulfilled its mission. She had brought joy and beauty and faith into our hearts; she had comforted us in our hours of loneliness and despair; she had been the little cheerful builder of our home—and perhaps God needed her.

She continued to sleep for three days, only for those three days her sun porch was a bower of roses. On Memorial Day, Mother and I stood once more together beside a little mound where God had led us. Late that afternoon we returned to the home to which Marjorie had taken us. It had grown more lovely with the beauty which has been ours, because of her.

The End

Through the deaths of his two children and his wife 14 years before his own death, Edgar experienced heart-wrenching sorrow. However, as the following poems show, he continued to carry optimism and hope, even in hard times.

A Child of Mine

I will lend you, for a little time,
A child of mine, He said.
For you to love the while she lives,
And mourn for when she's dead.

It may be six or seven years,
Or twenty-two or three.
But will you, till I call her back,
Take care of her for Me?
She'll bring her charms to gladden you,
And should her stay be brief.
You'll have her lovely memories,
As solace for your grief.
I cannot promise she will stay,
Since all from earth return.
But there are lessons taught down there,
I want this child to learn.
I've looked the wide world over,
In search for teachers true.
And from the throngs that crowd life's lanes,
I have selected you.
Now will you give her all your love,
Nor think the labour vain.

Nor hate me when I come to call
And take her back again?

I fancied that I heard them say,
'Dear Lord, Thy will be done!'
For all the joys Thy child shall bring,
The risk of grief we'll run.
We'll shelter her with tenderness,
We'll love her while we may,
And for the happiness we've known,
Forever grateful stay.
But should the angels call for her,
Much sooner than we've planned.
We'll brave the bitter grief that comes,
And try to understand.

Since Jessie Died

We understand a lot of things we never did before,

And it seems that to each other Ma and I are meaning more.

I don't know how to say it, but since little Jessie died

We have learned that to be happy we must travel side by side.

You can share your joys and pleasures, but you never come to know

The depth there is in loving, till you've got a common woe.

We're past the hurt of fretting—we can talk about it now:

She slipped away so gently and the fever left her brow

So softly that we didn't know we'd lost her, but, instead,

We thought her only sleeping as we watched beside her bed.

Then the doctor, I remember, raised his head, as if to say

What his eyes had told already, and Ma fainted dead away.

Up to then I thought that money was the thing I ought to get;

And I fancied, once I had it, I should never have to fret.

But I saw that I had wasted precious hours in seeking wealth;

I had made a tidy fortune, but I couldn't buy her health.

And I saw this truth much clearer than I'd ever seen before:

That the rich man and the poor man have to let death through the door.

We're not half so keen for money as one time
    we used to be;
I am thinking more of mother and she's
    thinking more of me.
Now we spend more time together, and I know
    we're meaning more
To each other on life's journey, than we ever
    meant before.
It was hard to understand it! Oh, the dreary
    nights we've cried!
But we've found the depth of loving, since the
    day that Jessie died.

Marjorie

The house is as it was when she was here;
There's nothing changed at all about the place;
The books she loved to read are waiting near
As if to-morrow they would see her face;
Her room remains the way it used to be,
Here are the puzzles that she pondered on:
Yet since the angels called for Marjorie
The joyous spirit of the home has gone.

All things grew lovely underneath her touch,
The room was bright because it knew her smile;
From her the tiniest trinket gathered much,
The cheapest toy became a thing worth while;
Yet here are her possessions as they were,
No longer joys to set the eyes aglow;
To-day, as we, they seem to mourn for her,
And share the sadness that is ours to know.

Half sobbing now, we put her games away,
Because, dumb things, they cannot understand
Why never more shall Marjorie come to play,
And we have faith in God at our command.
These toys we smiled at once, now start our
    tears,
They seem to wonder why they lie so still,

They call her name, and will throughout the years—
God, strengthen us to bow unto Thy will.

Until She Died

Until she died we never knew
The beauty of our faith in God.
We'd seen the summer roses nod
And wither as the tempests blew,
Through many a spring we'd lived to see
The buds returning to the tree.

We had not felt the touch of woe;
What cares had come, had lightly flown;
Our burdens we had borne alone—
The need of God we did not know.
It seemed sufficient through the days
To think and act in worldly ways.

And then she closed her eyes in sleep;
She left us for a little while;
No more our lives would know her smile.
And oh, the hurt of it went deep!
It seemed to us that we must fall
Before the anguish of it all.

Our faith, which had not known the test,
Then blossomed with its comfort sweet,
Promised that some day we should meet
And whispered to us: 'He knows best.'
And when our bitter tears were dried,
We found our faith was glorified.

Chapter 6

Poems about Home

Like many of you reading this book, I didn't have a picture-perfect home during my childhood, although there were a tremendous number of blessings to be thankful for. Edgar Guest's poems often portray ideal homes, and that is, perhaps, one reason I love his poems so much—they are filled with the kind of hope and goodness that we all strive for in our homes.

A Song

Rough be the road and long,
Steep be the hills ahead,
Grant that my faith be strong,
Fearlessly let me tread.
After the day's hard test
Home—with its peaceful rest.

Heavy my burdens be,
Let me not falter though,
Soon I shall come to see
Home, where the roses grow.
Home, where the swallows nest,
Home, with its peaceful rest.

This grant to me at last,
When I have ceased to roam,
When all my cares are past,
I may be welcomed home,
Home, where is none distressed,
Home, with its peaceful rest.

The Path to Home

There's the mother at the doorway, and the children at the gate,
And the little parlor windows with the curtains white and straight.
There are shaggy asters blooming in the bed that lines the fence,
And the simplest of the blossoms seems of mighty consequence.
Oh, there isn't any mansion underneath God's starry dome
That can rest a weary pilgrim like the little place called home.

Men have sought for gold and silver; men have dreamed at night of fame;
In the heat of youth they've struggled for achievement's honored name;
But the selfish crowns are tinsel, and their shining jewels paste,
And the wine of pomp and glory soon grows bitter to the taste.
For there's never any laughter howsoever far you roam,
Like the laughter of the loved ones in the happiness of home.

The Home Builders

The world is filled with bustle and with selfishness and greed,
It is filled with restless people that are dreaming of a deed.
You can read it in their faces; they are dreaming of the day
When they'll come to fame and fortune and put all their cares away.
And I think as I behold them, though it's far indeed they roam,
They will never find contentment save they seek for it at home.

I watch them as they hurry through the surging lines of men,
Spurred to speed by grim ambition, and I know they're dreaming then.
They are weary, sick and footsore, but their goal seems far away,
And it's little they've accomplished at the ending of the day.
It is rest they're vainly seeking, love and laughter in the gloam,
But they'll never come to claim it, save they claim it here at home.

For the peace that is the sweetest isn't born of minted gold,
And the joy that lasts the longest and still lingers when we're old

Is no dim and distant pleasure—it is not to-morrow's prize,
It is not the end of toiling, or the rainbow of our sighs.
It is every day within us—all the rest is hippodrome—
And the soul that is the gladdest is the soul that builds a home.

They are fools who build for glory! They are fools who pin their hopes
On the come and go of battles or some vessel's slender ropes.
They shall sicken and shall wither and shall never peace attain
Who believe that real contentment only men victorious gain.
For the only happy toilers under earth's majestic dome
Are the ones who find their glories in the little spot called home.

Grass and Children

I used to want a lovely lawn, a level patch of green,
For I have marveled many times at those that I have seen,
And in my early dreams of youth the home that I should keep

Possessed a lawn of beauty rare, a velvet carpet deep,
But I have changed my mind since then—for then I didn't know
That where the feet of children run the grass can never grow.

Now I might own a lovely lawn, but I should have to say
To all the little ones about, "Go somewhere else to play!"
And I should have to stretch a wire about my garden space
And make the home where gladness reigns, a most forbidding place.
By stopping all the merriment which now is ours to know,
In time, beyond the slightest doubt, the tender grass would grow.

But oh, I want the children near, and so I never say,
When they are romping around the home, "Go somewhere else to play!"
And though my lawn seems poorly kept, and many a spot is bare,
I'd rather see, than growing grass, the youngsters happy there.
I've put aside the dream I had in that far long ago—
I'd rather have a playground than a place for grass to grow.

The Toy-Strewn Home

Give me the house where the toys are strewn,
Where the dolls are asleep in the chairs,
Where the building blocks and the toy balloon
And the soldiers guard the stairs.
Let me step in a house where the tiny cart
With the horses rules the floor,
And rest comes into my weary heart,
For I am at home once more.

Give me the house with the toys about,
With the battered old train of cars,
The box of paints and the books left out,
And the ship with her broken spars.
Let me step in a house at the close of day
That is littered with children's toys,
And dwell once more in the haunts of play,
With the echoes of by-gone noise.

Give me the house where the toys are seen,
The house where the children romp,
And I'll happier be than man has been
'Neath the gilded dome of pomp.
Let me see the litter of bright-eyed play
Strewn over the parlor floor,
And the joys I knew in a far-off day
Will gladden my heart once more.

Whoever has lived in a toy-strewn home,
Though feeble he be and gray,
Will yearn, no matter how far he roam,
For the glorious disarray
Of the little home with its littered floor
That was his in the by-gone days;
And his heart will throb as it throbbed before,
When he rests where a baby plays.

A Warm House and a Ruddy Fire

A warm house and a ruddy fire,
To what more can man aspire?
Eyes that shine with love aglow,
Is there more for man to know?

Whether home be rich or poor,
If contentment mark the door
He who finds it good to live
Has the best that life can give.

This the end of mortal strife!
Peace at night to sweeten life,
Rest when mind and body tire,
At contentment's ruddy fire.

Rooms where merry songs are sung,
Happy old and glorious young;
These, if perfect peace be known,
Both the rich and poor must own.

A warm house and a ruddy fire,
These the goals of all desire,
These the dream of every man
Since God spoke and life began.

The Home-Wrecker

Mischievous and full of fun,
Eyes that sparkle like the sun;
Mouth that's always in a smile,
Hands in trouble all the while.
Tugging this and tugging that,

Nothing that you don't get at,
Nothing that you do not do,
Roguish little tyke of two.

Prying round the house you go,
Everything you want to know,
Everything you want to see,
Bunch of curiosity.
Nothing's safe with you about,
Nothing you don't ferret out.
'No! No's!' do not hinder you,
Roguish little tyke of two.

All day long you tear and break,
Ruin follows in your wake,
Just as though the tables are
Made for little feet to mar;
Just as though I spend my cash

For pottery for you to smash;
You're destructive through and through,
Roguish little tyke of two.

Hands and feet are never still,
Ink you think is made to spill;
On from this to that you pass
To the sound of falling glass.
Cups, you think, were made to throw
On the hardwood floor below.
Gleefully their wreck you view,
Roguish little tyke of two.

But I'd rather have it so,
Than the home I used to know;
Rather have you crash and break,
Leaving ruin in your wake;
Rather have you tug and tear

Till the place is worn and bare,
Than the childless home I knew,
Roguish little tyke of two.

Home

It takes a heap o' livin' in a house t' make it home,
A heap o' sun an' shadder, an' ye sometimes have t' roam
Afore ye really 'preciate the things ye lef' behind,
An' hunger fer 'em somehow, with 'em allus on yer mind.
It don't make any differunce how rich ye get t' be,
How much yer chairs an' tables cost, how great yer luxury;
It ain't home t' ye, though it be the palace of a king,
Until somehow yer soul is sort o' wrapped round everything.

Home ain't a place that gold can buy or get up in a minute;
Afore it's home there's got t' be a heap o' livin' in it;
Within the walls there's got t' be some babies born, and then
Right there ye've got t' bring 'em up t' women good, an' men;
And gradjerly, as time goes on, ye find ye wouldn't part
With anything they ever used—they've grown into yer heart:
The old high chairs, the playthings, too, the little shoes they wore
Ye hoard; an' if ye could ye'd keep the thumbmarks on the door.

Ye've got t' weep t' make it home, ye've got t' sit an' sigh

An' watch beside a loved one's bed, an' know that Death is nigh;

An' in the stillness o' the night t' see Death's angel come,

An' close the eyes o' her that smiled, an' leave her sweet voice dumb.

Fer these are scenes that grip the heart, an' when yer tears are dried,

Ye find the home is dearer than it was, an' sanctified;

An' tuggin' at ye always are the pleasant memories

O' her that was an' is no more—ye can't escape from these.

Ye've got t' sing an' dance fer years, ye've got t' romp an' play,

An' learn t' love the things ye have by usin' 'em each day;

Even the roses 'round the porch must blossom year by year

Afore they 'come a part o' ye, suggestin' someone dear

Who used t' love 'em long ago, an' trained 'em jes' t' run

The way they do, so's they would get the early mornin' sun;

Ye've got t' love each brick an' stone from cellar up t' dome:

It takes a heap o' livin' in a house t' make it home.

The Things They Mustn't Touch

Been down to the art museum an' looked at a thousand things,

The bodies of ancient mummies an' the treasures of ancient kings,

An' some of the walls were lovely, but some of the things weren't much,
But all had a rail around 'em, an' all wore a sign 'Don't touch.'

Now maybe an art museum needs guards and a warning sign
An' the hands of the folks should never paw over its treasures fine;
But I noticed the rooms were chilly with all the joys they hold,
An' in spite of the lovely pictures, I'd say that the place is cold.

An' somehow I got to thinkin' of many a home I know
Which is kept like an art museum, an' merely a place for show;
They haven't railed off their treasures or posted up signs or such,
But all of the children know it—there's a lot that they mustn't touch.

It's hands off the grand piano, keep out of the finest chair,
Stay out of the stylish parlor, don't run on the shiny stair;
You may look at the velvet curtains which hang in the stately hall,
But always and ever remember, they're not to be touched at all.

'Don't touch!' for an art museum, is proper enough, I know,
But my children's feet shall scamper wherever they want to go,
And I want no rare possessions or a joy which has cost so much,
From which I must bar the children and tell them they 'mustn't touch.'

Our Little House

I'd like to have them think of me
As one with whom they liked to be;
I'd like to make my home so fair
That they would all be happy there;
To have them think, when life is done,
That here they had their finest fun.

Within these walls with love aglow,
They live to-morrow's "Long Ago."
Nor is the time so far away
When now shall be their yesterday,
And they shall turn once more to see
The little home which used to be.

When comes that time I want them then
To wish they could be here again;
I want their memories to be
A picture of a kindly me,
To have them say how very glad
Their youthful lives were made by dad.

I want them to recall this place
As one of charm and tender grace,
To love these walls of calm content
Wherein their youthful years were spent,
And feel through each succeeding year,
They lived their happiest moments here.

I feel I shall have failed unless
This house shall shelter happiness.
Save they shall find their truest mirth
Around their father's humble hearth,
And here life's finest joys attain,
I shall have lived my life in vain.

When Day Is Done

When day is done and the night slips down,
And I've turned my back on the busy town,
And come once more to the welcome gate
Where the roses nod and the children wait,
I tell myself as I see them smile
That life is good and its tasks worth while.

When day is done and I've come once more
To my quiet street and the friendly door,
Where the Mother reigns and the children play
And the kettle sings in the old-time way,
I throw my coat on a near-by chair
And say farewell to my pack of care.

When day is done, all the hurt and strife
And the selfishness and the greed of life,
Are left behind in the busy town;
I've ceased to worry about renown
Or gold or fame, and I'm just a dad,
Content to be with his girl and lad.

Whatever the day has brought of care,
Here love and laughter are mine to share,
Here I can claim what the rich desire—
Rest and peace by a ruddy fire,
The welcome words which the loved ones speak
And the soft caress of a baby's cheek.

When day is done and I reach my gate,
I come to a realm where there is no hate,
For here, whatever my worth may be,
Are those who cling to their faith in me;
And with love on guard at my humble door,
I have all that the world has struggled for.

Treasures

Some folks I know, when friends drop in
To visit for awhile and chin,
Just lead them round the rooms and halls
And show them pictures on their walls,
And point to rugs and tapestries
The works of men across the seas;
Their loving cups they show with pride,
To eyes that soon are stretching wide
With wonder at the treasures rare
That have been bought and gathered there.

But when folks come to call on me,
I've no such things for them to see.
No picture on my walls is great;
I have no ancient family plate;
No tapestry of rare design
Or costly woven rugs are mine;
I have no loving cup to show,
Or strange and valued curio;
But if my treasures they would see,
I bid them softly follow me.

And then I lead them up the stairs
Through trains of cars and Teddy bears,
And to a little room we creep
Where both my youngsters lie asleep,
Close locked in one another's arms.
I let them gaze upon their charms,
I let them see the legs of brown
Curled up beneath a sleeping gown,
And whisper in my happiness:
"Behold the treasures I possess."

Living Beauties

I never knew, until they went,
How much their laughter really meant
I never knew how much the place
Depended on each little face;
How barren home could be and drear
Without its living beauties here.

I never knew that chairs and books
Could wear such sad and solemn looks!
That rooms and halls could be at night
So still and drained of all delight.
This home is now but brick and board
Where bits of furniture are stored.

I used to think I loved each shelf
And room for what it was itself.
And once I thought each picture fine
Because I proudly called it mine.
But now I know they mean no more
Than art works hanging in a store.

Until they went away to roam
I never knew what made it home.
But I have learned that all is base,
However wonderful the place
And decked with costly treasures, rare,
Unless the living joys are there.

Chapter 7

Faith

Faith in God played a large role in Edgar Guest's life and his poetry. He said, "You have asked me the relations of religion to poetry. They are close together. My opinion is that a man must have some religion, perhaps 'faith' is a better term—faith in a Higher Power, faith to feel that this life is not all there is. Faith is necessary if one is to find any real beauty in living. . . . A poet must keep in touch with spiritual realities. He must have spiritual fuel."[1]

Woven through Edgar's volumes of poetry is a humble and steadfast faith in God that, indeed, shows the real beauty in living. Edgar saw God in the little, everyday things and in the monumental things, such as death.

---

1. Edward H. Cotton, "Edgar A. Guest, the Fireside Poet," 1161.

A Package of Seeds

I paid a dime for a package of seeds
And the clerk tossed them out with a flip.
"We've got 'em assorted for every man's needs,"
He said with a smile on his lip.
"Pansies and poppies and asters and peas!
Ten cents a package and pick as you please!"

Now seeds are just dimes to the man in the store
And dimes are the things he needs;
And I've been to buy them in seasons before,
But have thought of them merely as seeds.
But it flashed through my mind as I took them this time
"You have purchased a miracle here for a dime!"

"You've a dime's worth of power no man can create,
You've a dime's worth of life in your hand!
You've a dime's worth of mystery, destiny, fate,
Which the wisest cannot understand.
In this bright little package, now isn't it odd?
You've a dime's worth of something known only to God."

Bulb Planting Time

Last night he said the dead were dead
And scoffed my faith to scorn;
I found him at a tulip bed
When I passed by at morn.

'O ho!' said I, 'the frost is near
And mist is on the hills,
And yet I find you planting here
Tulips and daffodils.'

''Tis time to plant them now,' he said,
'If they shall bloom in Spring';
'But every bulb,' said I, 'seems dead,
And such an ugly thing.'

'The pulse of life I cannot feel,
The skin is dried and brown.
Now look!' a bulb beneath my heel
I crushed and trampled down.

In anger then he said to me:
'You've killed a lovely thing;
A scarlet blossom that would be
Some morning in the Spring.'

'Last night a greater sin was thine,'
To him I slowly said;
'You trampled on the dead of mine
And told me they are dead.'

When Sorrow Comes

When sorrow comes, as come it must,
In God a man must place his trust.
There is no power in mortal speech
The anguish of his soul to reach,
No voice, however sweet and low,
Can comfort him or ease the blow.

He cannot from his fellowmen
Take strength that will sustain him then.
With all that kindly hands will do,
And all that love may offer, too,
He must believe throughout the test
That God has willed it for the best.

We who would be his friends are dumb;
Words from our lips but feebly come;
We feel, as we extend our hands,
That one Power only understands
And truly knows the reason why
So beautiful a soul must die.

We realize how helpless then
Are all the gifts of mortal men.
No words which we have power to say
Can take the sting of grief away—
That Power which marks the sparrow's fall
Must comfort and sustain us all.

When sorrow comes, as come it must,
In God a man must place his trust.
With all the wealth which he may own,
He cannot meet the test alone,
And only he may stand serene
Who has a faith on which to lean.

Silence

I did not argue with the man,
It seemed a waste of words.
He gave to chance the wondrous plan
That gave sweet song to birds.

He gave to force the wisdom wise
That shaped the honeybee,
And made the useful butterflies
So beautiful to see.

And as we walked 'neath splendid trees
Which cast a friendly shade,
He said: 'Such miracles as these
By accident were made.'

Too well I know what accident
And chance and force disclose
To think blind fury could invent
The beauty of a rose.

I let him talk and answered not.
I merely thought it odd
That he could view a garden plot
And not believe in God.

Royce Howes wrote: "As with his appreciation of good books and his ardor to learn, Eddie Guest attributes his lifelong belief in worship and in the tenets taught where worshippers gather to the influence of his mother."[2]

2. Royce Howes and John S. Knight, *Edgar A. Guest: A Biography.*

In 1925, Edgar Guest wrote an extended essay titled *What My Religion Means to Me*. Edgar was a Freemason and a member of the Episcopal Church, but his insights in this essay strike truths close to the hearts of all Christians.

What My Religion Means to Me

Religion has been the greatest single influence in my life. At forty-three, I can look back and see that but for the spiritual teaching and help which I received from my mother, the achievements which have strengthened and comforted and pleased me most could never have been. Without that religious belief which she impressed upon me, I am certain that I should not be where I am today. I should not have the friends which are mine, nor the place which I occupy. I should be somewhere back in the desert of doubt and skepticism, groping and struggling along, seeking material success with only the poor tools of my ability.

Without my religion, I should have made enemies where I have gathered friends.

Without my religion I should have gone down where I have climbed up; I should have been sordid where I have found joy in being sentimental; I should have been shunned where I have been welcomed, and although I might have made money and saved some portion of it, I am sure that I should have done many things which would have been to me a shame and a regret.

Without my religion, I should have suffered a loss in self-respect and in the esteem of others.

I am convinced that religion is necessary to worthwhile achievement.

I want Bud, my boy, to know this. The sooner any young man discovers that belief in God and belief in his own divine purpose are vital to his career, the better it will be for him. I would rather die leaving nothing to my boy but his religion, than to die leaving him a fortune, with no religion.

If I can but impress upon him, as my mother impressed upon me, the fact that God has given him a soul to be his for all eternity, that he has been blessed with divine powers to beautify and glorify that soul; if I can give to him the sure belief in a Supreme Being, I shall not have to worry about his future. He will be safe against temptation. He will be able to see crooks and liars and cheats prosper temporarily, and still retain his own honor. With that faith he can be manly, self-reliant, independent, humor-loving, artistic, athletic, friendly, and whatsoever he wills to be. The boy who has faith in God will have faith in himself.

The football player with a religion is a better player than the boy without one. The business man with a real, live, earnest religion is a better businessman than the scoffing non-believer. All the great men of nearly all the ages have had a religion.

But with Bud's own faith I want him also to have respect for the religion of others. His soul can never become truly great by warping it into the straight-jacket of the bigot. Religion has suffered most from two classes of people—the hypocrites and the bigots.

The bigots have stained their conception of Christianity with bloodshed and crimes; the hypocrites have made religion appear ridiculous and dishonest. It is difficult to guess which has done the more harm. The bigots have driven men away from the church; the hypocrites have kept countless numbers out of it.

I want Bud to know that he can have his religion without being a mollycoddle. He can keep his manhood and his faith side by side. He can laugh and be religious; he can play football, swim, go fishing, and hunting; in short, he can express in his own way the joy of being alive, and at the same time be religious. I can see nothing in the church or its teachings which should change a naturally robust, healthy-minded, joyous human being into a pasty-faced, smug-smiling, hand-stroking, intolerant creature, neither all man nor all woman.

Nothing has hurt the church more, in my opinion, than the fear among the young people that religion would put an end to laughter and amusement. The old-fashioned church entertainment was a nightmare of boredom. It was reckoned almost a sin to laugh in the vicinity of a church.

Hypocrisy has dealt more than one foul blow to the church. The saintly hymn-singing person of the Sabbath who spent the weekdays in anything but Christian business practices has been an enemy and a hindrance to religion. He has made cynics and scoffers of our youth.

The religious fanatic and the religious grouch have been too much in the limelight, although they are not true types of the Christian religion. They have unconsciously made the teaching of religion most difficult for its best and manliest leaders. They have built a wall of prejudice which still exists, against which the real people within struggle in vain, and over which the young people without disdainfully refuse to climb.

I did take out of that little church in Detroit, which stood for years at the corner of Cass Avenue and High Street, a faith in God and life eternal which has sustained and protected me through all the trials and temptations which the years have brought. Perhaps, after all, that was the purpose of those ponderously heavy doctrinal sermons which oftentimes were over my head and far beyond my youthful understanding.

And now for an inventory of my religious experiences. I am satisfied beyond the slightest doubt that whatever good habits I have acquired I owe to my religion, and whatever bad habits and shortcomings and failings I have, I owe to grosser and more material influences.

Out of my religion have come the verses of mine which have had the widest appeal.

I owe to my religion my home and the peace within it.

I owe to my religion my ability to make friends and keep them.

I owe to it whatever of patience has been mine and whatever steadfastness of purpose I have displayed.

I owe to it my powers of understanding, for it was from my mother and her religious teachings I caught my first glimpse of the great brotherhood of man.

And it has all been so simple, and so practical. It has not changed my nature nor altered in the least my manner. It has regulated my conduct, but it has never kept me from a sport in which it was proper to indulge, nor has it kept me out of a business venture in which it was honest to engage.

I have met and walked and talked with all manner of men. I have laughed with the loudest, joked with the coarsest; visited as a reporter the vicious and the vile, and have done it without losing their respect or my own.

I have been neither a mollycoddle nor a brute. I have preached religion to no one nor have I tried to alter any man's religious opinions. I have tried never to be a wet blanket on the fire of any man's pleasure. I have made just a few rules for myself, and none for my neighbor. I have tried to keep my religion, my belief in God, and my faith in eternity, as a restraint for me alone.

I have not been what is called a regular church-goer. I have never been a deacon or a warden or a pillar. As a boy, I pumped the church organ twice every Sunday for two or three years, and once in a spirit of mischief I let the wind die out, to the utter destruction of the anthem. It was something I had secretly wanted to do. I thought it would be funny to desert the organist in the middle of his masterpiece!

The temptation to make that experiment was irresistible. On three or four occasions I let the wind die down until the little indicator was almost at its last notch, but my courage failed me. At the last second I swung the bellows stick viciously up and down and saved the day for the organist.

But the time came when I simply had to go through with it. I ceased pumping, and sat back and awaited results. They came speedily enough. Soon the organ flattened out in one long, dismal wail! I could hear the organist's fingers striking the ivory keys, but there was no other sound. The choir tried to continue with the anthem, but the congregation began to titter and the titters increased to audible laughter. There were frantic calls for me on the electric buzzer, and the next week there was a new boy pumping the organ.

Thus ended my connection with the church in an official capacity. I continued to attend, but my place thereafter was in the family pew, where the family could keep an eye upon me.

A few years later I became a reporter on the Detroit "Free Press," and my duty on Sundays was to report news about the churches. Within a few months I had sat beneath the teachers of nearly every religion and creed. I had attended services in orthodox and reformed Jewish synagogues; masses in Catholic churches; baptisms in the Baptist churches; revivals in Methodist churches, and so on through the long list of them all.

I had been in cathedrals and little frame mission houses, and I made the discovery that all of them, from the greatest to the humblest, were trying for the same result—to do good. I have never been in a church in which I have ever heard a minister attempt by his utterances to degrade a man or lower his standards or ideals.

In the course of time I made still another discovery: My visits to these churches had enriched me with various friendships. Rabbi Leo M. Franklin has been my friend almost from the day of his arrival in Detroit, more than twenty years ago. The same is true of Bishop Gallagher, of the Catholic Church, and Bishop Henderson, of the Methodist Church. I counted among my friends the priests and ministers and the laymen of all the denominations and almost all the known faiths of the country.

What a loss would be mine if I should let religion build a wall of prejudice about me!

What if I were to restrict my friends to those of my own particular little faith?

I might as well determine to walk only with people who wear bow ties like myself, or gray suits. I don't like pumpkin pie, but if I shunned all the people who do, I should have to give up the company of my wife and children, who are very fond of it.

So in those early reportorial days of mine I added to my religion a resolution not to be a bigot. I determined in advance never to like or dislike any human being because of his religion.

That which gives comfort to another, I decided, I would respect. The man whose belief in God is strong enough to lead him to go to any church has that kinship with me which makes him a brother.

He may lose my friendship by wrong doing; may lose my respect by vicious habits and crooked dealing; I may shun him because he is loud and vulgar and distasteful; I may despise him because I have found him to be a liar or a cheat or self-centered to the extreme, a faithless husband and an unkind father, but I shall never censure him for his faith nor deny him my good will because of his religion.

I have always tried to be tolerant. Clinging fast to my own religion I have endeavored, as far as it was within my power to do so, to support and respect all churches.

Bud, my boy, be tolerant of your brother's faith. Nothing that he learns in his church will degrade him or you. No religion will teach him to cheat you or harm you or lead you astray. If you shall find him unworthy of your trust and your companionship, it will not be because of his church but in spite of it. You may be sure that he got his vicious habits and his mean practices elsewhere. He is not bad because he is Catholic, Jew or Protestant; he is bad because he has deserted his religion.

One of the most pleasing little bits which have ever appeared in print about me was published a few years ago by a Catholic weekly which is circulated through Michigan. An inquiring correspondent wrote to the editor this question:

"Is Edgar A. Guest a Catholic?"

The editor printed his reply in about these words:

"Edgar A. Guest is not a Catholic. We understand that he is an Episcopalian; but we should like to say to our inquirer that all Catholics who know him consider him their friend."

The further I go up the hill of life the more tolerant I become.

Religion pays. Get this straight, Bud—crooks and highwaymen and gangsters and rioters, and all the lowest elements of mankind, are seldom or never religious. But Presidents, and statesmen, and great lawyers and great artists, and the leaders in all the trades and professions, usually are.

The people who go to the churches are the best people of the community. Forget the smug hymn-singing hypocrite and the narrow little bigot, and remember only this fact: If you hope for the best; if you would make the most of yourself and your opportunity; if you would win honor and good will and the world's esteem, you will need all the courage and all the inspiration and all the strength which your religion can give you. Without religion you will never be as great a man as you would be with it.

Bud, you can keep your faith in God and follow any profession you may choose. It will not restrict your opportunity nor become an obstacle to your ambition. It will not deprive you of a single manly friend. You will not have to associate with sissies to be religious. You can be red-blooded and virile and strong. If you should choose to become a prize fighter—I hope you won't—I should want you to cling to your religion. You would be a better prize fighter for your faith. Your religion would keep you from striking a foul blow. It would make you a generous victor and a gracious loser. It would give you character and demeanor which would make you popular with your spectators. You would lift prize fighting to a higher level by your example.

You may not believe it now, but someday you will discover that the good men in all trades and all professions and in all places have a religion. They don't all go to church every Sunday. They don't all wear black clothes and somber expressions on their countenances. They don't despise decent fun. They go to baseball games and theatres and dances; they play cards, and they have their little faults and weaknesses, but in the main they are sustained in trial by an unfaltering faith in God, and they keep their souls and lives as clean as possible for the life eternal which surely is to come.

The man who is in any way worthwhile has a religion of some sort.

Frank Reilly, my publisher, and I were sitting together one day a few weeks ago. Suddenly he turned to me and said:

"Eddie, do you know where your greatest strength lies?"

"No," I answered. "Where is it?"

"It's in the religious note you strike in your verses," he replied earnestly. "In all the letters which come to us regarding your work there is always mention of some particular little bit which has to do with your faith."

"I'm glad to hear you speak of it in that way," I said. "In other words, you mean that my religion has made me a little more valuable to myself and to you."

"I wasn't thinking of it in those words," Reilly continued, "but I suppose that is precisely it. With your religion you undoubtedly are a better man for us than you would be without it. I should say that we sell many thousands more of your books because you are, at heart, deeply religious, than we should sell if you were not."

"Then, Frank," I said, "my mother was right when she taught me to believe in God, and I have been right in sticking to that belief. It has actually paid me in dollars and cents. All the time, I was simply writing the thoughts I have had and have come to believe, which sprang out of my mother's early training and counsel, and those things which have seemed so true to others. But I wasn't thinking of profit or popularity when I did those bits."

"No." he answered. "That is probably the reason you have earned both. But what do you suppose you were thinking of?"

"Nothing but doing the best possible bit of work I could do that day and doing it as quickly as possible. It is more than probable that I was eager to get out on the golf course."

And so I rejoice in my religion and am grateful to it. It has strengthened and sustained me in times of sorrow; it has opened the door to many fellowships; it has made my speech less bitter; it has widened my field of labor; it has kept me straight when I have been tempted; it has led me to read many books I should otherwise have missed, and has brought to my door countless friends I should otherwise have lost. And, finally, as Frank Reilly has informed me, it has increased my reputation and my royalties.

But above and beyond all that, it has paid me peace of mind.

Chapter 8

Friendship

Friendship was something that Edgar Guest deeply valued. In his poems and in his essay "The Art of Making Friends," he shares some profound advice about why and how to make and keep friends. Some excerpts of his essay are shared here.

To have friends, a man must first be a friend. He who has many friends has been a friend to many. The art of friendship is self-acquired. Men go to schools to learn to paint, and carve, and draw, and write; there are dancing schools and finishing schools for girls where etiquette and deportment are taught for a price; there are crafts and many arts; but the greatest of all the arts—that of making friends—comes to a man from within, and only when he makes the patient effort to deserve it.

Friendship must be a lifetime habit. The most important thing you can teach a boy is how to get along with his fellows. Nature, I suppose, has something to do with our likes and dislikes; our strengths and weaknesses. But the control of our conduct is in our own hands. He who comes to the end of life's road with no devoted friends has only himself to blame.

Is an ill temper admired by anyone? Not at all. Then put away your silly fits of rage. Do you like a lad who cheats to win? You don't? Then never be a cheat yourself. Do you like to hear slurs and sneers and smart words that sting and burn? No. Then think twice before you utter them. Do you like to be warmly welcomed? Do you like to receive the little attentions which are evidences of thoughtfulness and respect for you? You do. Then bestow them always on others, particularly those who might not rightfully expect them. This is the road to friendship.

It's an art to be able to make people happy. It's an art to be genuine and real and solid and worthwhile. It's an art to dismiss everything that is petty and trivial and insignificant, and play the host and friend. Making friends is an art. Keeping them is a greater one.

The Way to Make Friends

The way to make friends is as easy
As breathing the fresh morning air;
It isn't an art to be studied
Alone by the men who can spare
The time from their every day labors,
To ponder on classical lore,
It never is taught in a college
And it isn't a trick or a chore.

The way to make friends is to be one,
To smile at the stranger you meet,
To think cheerful thoughts and to speak them
Aloud to the people you greet.
To hold your hand out to a brother,
And cheerfully say: 'Howdy-do,'
In a way that he'll know that you mean it,

That's all that's expected of you.
Be honest in all of your dealings,
Be true to your word and your home,
And you will make friends, never doubt it,
Wherever you happen to roam.
Condemn not the brother who falters,
Nor fawn on the rich and the great.
Speak kindly to all who approach you,
And give up all whining at fate.

The Kindly Neighbor

I have a kindly neighbor, one who stands
Beside my gate and chats with me awhile,
Gives me the glory of his radiant smile
And comes at times to help with willing hands.
No station high or rank this man commands,
He, too, must trudge, as I, the long day's mile;
And yet, devoid of pomp or gaudy style,
He has a worth exceeding stocks or lands.

To him I go when sorrow's at my door,
On him I lean when burdens come my way,
Together oft we talk our trials o'er
And there is warmth in each good-night we say.
A kindly neighbor! Wars and strife shall end
When man has made the man next door his friend.

The Obligation of Friendship

You ought to be fine for the sake of the folks
Who think you are fine.
If others have faith in you doubly you're bound

To stick to the line.

It's not only on you that dishonor descends:

You can't hurt yourself without hurting your friends.

You ought to be true for the sake of the folks

Who believe you are true.

You never should stoop to a deed that your friends

Think you wouldn't do.

If you're false to yourself, be the blemish but small,

You have injured your friends; you've been false to them all.

For friendship, my boy, is a bond between men

That is founded on truth:

It believes in the best of the ones that it loves.

Whether old man or youth;

And the stern rule it lays down for me and for you

Is to be what our friends think we are, through and through.

To an Old Friend

When we have lived our little lives and wandered all their byways through,

When we've seen all that we shall see and finished all that we must do,

When we shall take one backward look off yonder where our journey ends,

I pray that you shall be as glad as I shall be that we were friends.

Time was we started out to find the treasures and the joys of life;

We sought them in the land of gold through many days of bitter strife.

When we were young we yearned for fame; in search of joy we went afar,
Only to learn how very cold and distant all the strangers are.

When we have met all we shall meet and know what destiny has planned,
I shall rejoice in that last hour that I have known your friendly hand;
I shall go singing down the way off yonder as my sun descends
As one who's had a happy life, made glorious by the best of friends.

A Friend's Greeting

I'd like to be the sort of friend that you have been to me;
I'd like to be the help that you've been always glad to be;
I'd like to mean as much to you each minute of the day
As you have meant, old friend of mine, to me along the way.

I'd like to do the big things and the splendid things for you,
To brush the gray from out your skies and leave them only blue;

I'd like to say the kindly things that I so oft have heard,
And feel that I could rouse your soul the way that mine you've stirred.

I'd like to give you back the joy that you have given me,
Yet that were wishing you a need I hope will never be;
I'd like to make you feel as rich as I, who travel on
Undaunted in the darkest hours with you to lean upon.

I'm wishing at this Christmas time that I could but repay
A portion of the gladness that you've strewn along my way;
And could I have one wish this year, this only would it be:
I'd like to be the sort of friend that you have been to me.

Friends

Ain't it fine when things are going
Topsy-turvy and askew
To discover someone showing
Good old-fashioned faith in you?

Ain't it good when life seems dreary
And your hopes about to end,
Just to feel the handclasp cheery
Of a fine old loyal friend?

Gosh! one fellow to another
Means a lot from day to day,
Seems we're living for each other
In a friendly sort of way.

When a smile or cheerful greetin'
Means so much to fellows sore,
Seems we ought to keep repeatin'
Smiles an' praises more an' more.

Success

I hold no dream of fortune vast,
Nor seek undying fame.
I do not ask when life is past
That many know my name.

I may not own the skill to rise
To glory's topmost height,
Nor win a place among the wise,
But I can keep the right.

And I can live my life on earth
Contented to the end,
If but a few shall know my worth
And proudly call me friend.

The Fellowship of Books

I care not who the man may be,
    Nor how his tasks may fret him,
Nor where he fares, nor how his cares
    And troubles may beset him,
If books have won the love of him,
    Whatever fortune hands him,
He'll always own, when he's alone,
    A friend who understands him.

Though other friends may come and go,
    And some may stoop to treason,
His books remain, through loss or gain,
    And season after season
The faithful friends for every mood,
    His joy and sorrow sharing,
For old time's sake, they'll lighter make
    The burdens he is bearing.

Oh, he has counsel at his side,
    And wisdom for his duty,
And laughter gay for hours of play,
    And tenderness and beauty,
And fellowship divinely rare,
    True friends who never doubt him,
Unchanging love, and God above,
    Who keeps good books about him.

The Test

You can brag about the famous men you know;
You may boast about the great men you have met,
Parsons, eloquent and wise; stars in histrionic skies;
Millionaires and navy admirals, and yet
Fame and power and wealth and glory vanish fast;
They are lusters that were never made to stick,
And the friends worth-while and true, are the happy smiling few
Who come to call upon you when you're sick.

You may think it very fine to know the great;
You may glory in some leader's words of praise;
You may tell with eyes aglow of the public men you know,
But the true friends seldom travel glory's ways,
And the day you're lying ill, lonely, pale and keeping still,
With a fevered pulse, that's beating double quick,
Then it is you must depend on the old-familiar friend

To come to call upon you when you're sick.
It is pleasing to receive a great man's nod,
And it's good to know the big men of the land,
But the test of friendship true, isn't merely: 'Howdy-do?'
And a willingness to shake you by the hand.
If you want to know the friends who love you best,
And the faithful from the doubtful you would pick,
It is not a mighty task; of yourself you've but to ask:
'Does he come to call upon me when I'm sick?'

The Making of a Friend

We nodded as we passed each day
And smiled and went along our way;
I knew his name, and he knew mine,
But neither of us made a sign
That we possessed a common tie;
We barely spoke as we passed by.

How fine he was I never guessed.
The splendid soul within his breast
I never saw. From me were hid
The many kindly deeds he did.
His gentle ways I didn't know,
Or I'd have claimed him long ago.

Then trouble came to me one day,
And he was first to come and say
The cheering words I longed to hear.
He offered help, and standing near
I felt our lives in sorrow blend—
My neighbor had become my friend.

How many smiles from day to day
I've missed along my narrow way;
How many kindly words I've lost,
What joy has my indifference cost?

This glorious friend that now I know,
Would have been friendly years ago.

Be a Friend

Be a friend. You don't need money;
Just a disposition sunny;
Just the wish to help another
Get along some way or other;
Just a kindly hand extended
Out to one who's unbefriended;
Just the will to give or lend,
This will make you someone's friend.

Be a friend. You don't need glory.
Friendship is a simple story.
Pass by trifling errors blindly,
Gaze on honest effort kindly,

Cheer the youth who's bravely trying,
Pity him who's sadly sighing;
Just a little labor spend
On the duties of a friend.

Be a friend. The pay is bigger
(Though not written by a figure)
Than is earned by people clever
In what's merely self-endeavor.
You'll have friends instead of neighbors
For the profits of your labors;
You'll be richer in the end
Than a prince, if you're a friend.

Kindness

One never knows
How far a word of kindness goes;
One never sees
How far a smile of friendship flees.
Down, through the years,
The deed forgotten reappears.

One kindly word
The souls of many here has stirred.
Man goes his way
And tells with every passing day,
Until life's end:
'Once unto me he played the friend.'

We cannot say
What lips are praising us to-day.
We cannot tell
Whose prayers ask God to guard us well.
But kindness lives
Beyond the memory of him who gives.

Chapter 9

Character

A friend once wrote of Edgar Guest: "He never wrote a line that Father had to skip when he read to the family."[1] Edgar was known for being upright and living the things that he taught. Even when increased fame came to him—a weekly national broadcast on radio and TV—Guest remained true to his values and principles.

What is true success and how does one achieve it?

What matters most in life? What character traits should we strive for? These are all topics that Guest addressed over and over again in his poems, sometimes with a serious tone and often with a playful humor, but always with a genuine heart.

Reward

Don't want medals on my breast,
Don't want all the glory,
I'm not worrying greatly lest
The world won't hear my story.
A chance to dream beside a stream
Where fish are biting free;
A day or two, 'neath skies of blue,
Is joy enough for me.

I do not ask a hoard of gold,
Nor treasures rich and rare;
I don't want all the joys to hold;
I only want a share.
Just now and then, away from men

---

1. "Edgar A. Guest Coming: Popular Poet to Appear in College Chapel Saturday Afternoon," *Our College Times*, October 3, 1923.

And all their haunts of pride,
If I can steal, with rod and reel,
I will be satisfied.

I'll gladly work my way through life;
I would not always play;
I only ask to quit the strife
For an occasional day.
If I can sneak from toil a week
To chum with stream and tree,
I'll fish away and smiling say
That life's been good to me.

The Few

The easy roads are crowded
And the level roads are jammed;
The pleasant little rivers
With the drifting folks are crammed.
But off yonder where it's rocky,
Where you get a better view,
You will find the ranks are thinning
And the travelers are few.

Where the going's smooth and pleasant
You will always find the throng,
For the many, more's the pity,
Seem to like to drift along.
But the steeps that call for courage,
And the task that's hard to do
In the end result in glory
For the never-wavering few.

The Gentle Gardener

I'd like to leave but daffodills to mark my little way,
To leave but tulips red and white behind me as I stray;
I'd like to pass away from earth and feel I'd left behind
But roses and forget-me-nots for all who come to find.

I'd like to sow the barren spots with all the flowers of earth,
To leave a path where those who come should find but gentle mirth;
And when at last I'm called upon to join the heavenly throng
I'd like to feel along my way I'd left no sign of wrong.

And yet the cares are many and the hours of toil are few;
There is not time enough on earth for all I'd like to do;
But, having lived and having toiled, I'd like the world to find
Some little touch of beauty that my soul had left behind.

Results and Roses

The man who wants a garden fair,
Or small or very big,
With flowers growing here and there,
Must bend his back and dig.

The things are mighty few on earth
That wishes can attain.
Whate'er we want of any worth
We've got to work to gain.

It matters not what goal you seek
Its secret here reposes:
You've got to dig from week to week
To get Results or Roses.

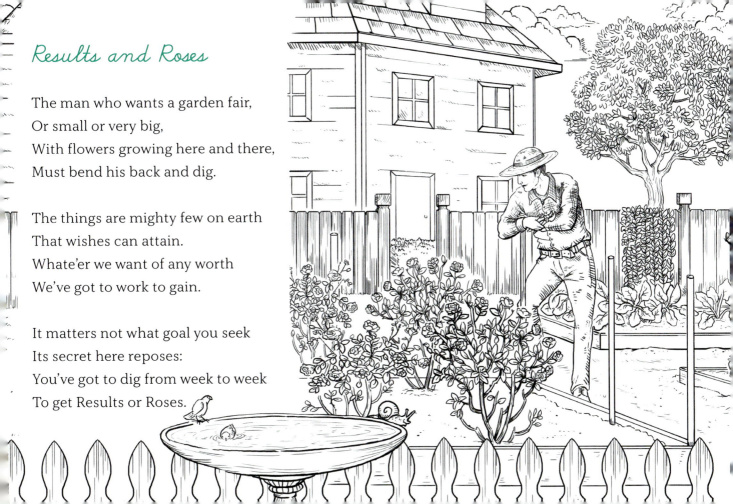

Failures

'Tis better to have tried in vain,
Sincerely striving for a goal,
Than to have lived upon the plain
An idle and a timid soul.

'Tis better to have fought and spent
Your courage, missing all applause,
Than to have lived in smug content
And never ventured for a cause.

For he who tries and fails may be
The founder of a better day;
Though never his the victory,
From him shall others learn the way.

Stick to It

Stick to it, boy,
Through the thick and the thin of it!
Work for the joy
That is born of the din of it.
Failures beset you,
But don't let them fret you;
Dangers are lurking,
But just keep on working.
If it's worth while and you're sure of the right of it,

Stick to it, boy, and make a real fight of it!
Stick to it, lad,
Be not frail and afraid of it;
Stand to the gad
For the man to be made of it.
Deaf to the sneering

And blind to the jeering,
Willing to master
The present disaster,
Stick to it, lad, through the trial and test of it,
Patience and courage will give you the best of it.

Stick to it, youth,
Be not sudden to fly from it;
This is the truth,
Triumph may not far lie from it
Dark is the morning
Before the sun's dawning,
Battered and sore of it
Bear a bit more of it,
Stick to it, even though blacker than ink it is,
Victory's nearer, perhaps, than you think it is!

The Happy Slow Thinker

Full many a time a thought has come
That had a bitter meaning in it.
And in the conversation's hum
I lost it ere I could begin it.

I've had it on my tongue to spring
Some poisoned quip that I thought clever;
Then something happened and the sting
Unuttered went, and died forever.

A lot of bitter thoughts I've had
To silence fellows and to flay 'em,
But next day always I've been glad
I wasn't quick enough to say 'em.

What I Call Living

The miser thinks he's living when he's hoarding up his gold;
The soldier calls it living when he's doing something bold;
The sailor thinks it living to be tossed upon the sea,
And upon this vital subject no two of us agree.
But I hold to the opinion, as I walk my way along,
That living's made of laughter and good-fellowship and song.

I wouldn't call it living always to be seeking gold,
To bank all the present gladness for the days when I'll be old.
I wouldn't call it living to spend all my strength for fame,
And forego the many pleasures which to-day are mine to claim.
I wouldn't for the splendor of the world set out to roam,
And forsake my laughing children and the peace I know at home.
Oh, the thing that I call living isn't gold or fame at all!

It's good-fellowship and sunshine, and it's roses by the wall;

It's evenings glad with music and a hearth fire that's ablaze,
And the joys which come to mortals in a thousand different ways.
It is laughter and contentment and the struggle for a goal;
It is everything that's needful in the shaping of a soul.

Think Happy Thoughts

Think sunshine all the day;
Refuse to let the trifling worries stay,
Crowd them with thoughts of laughter from your mind.
Think of the good, forget the bad you find,
Think of the sun behind the clouds; the blue
And not the gray skies that you view.
Think of the kindness not the meanness shown,
The true friends not the false ones you have known;
The joy and not the hatred of the strife,
The sweetness not the bitterness of life.
Think happy thoughts!

Think happy thoughts!
Think always of the best,
Think of the ones you love, not those that you detest;
Think of your victories and not your failures here,
The smile that pleased and not the hurtful sneer,
The kindly word and not the harsh word spoken,
The promise kept and not the promise broken;
The good that you have known and not the bad,
The happy days that were and not the sad;
Think of the rose and not the withered flower,
The beauty of the rainbow, not the shower.
Think happy thoughts!

Think happy thoughts!
This is true happiness!
That life is sad that feeds on its distress;
That mind is gloomy that subsists on gloom,
And is as dismal as a curtained room,

Where daily comes the sunshine, but to find
It cannot enter through the close-drawn blind.
Fling up the curtains of your mind today
And let the morning sunshine in to play;
Dwell on the joys and not the sorrows here,
Master your thoughts and you have mastered fear.
Think happy thoughts!

The Simple Things

I would not be too wise—so very wise
That I must sneer at simple songs and creeds,
And let the glare of wisdom blind my eyes
To humble people and their humble needs.

I would not care to climb so high that I
Could never hear the children at their play,
Could only see the people passing by,
And never hear the cheering words they say.

I would not know too much—too much to smile
At trivial errors of the heart and hand,
Nor be too proud to play the friend the while,
Nor cease to help and know and understand.

I would not care to sit upon a throne,
Or build my house upon a mountain-top,
Where I must dwell in glory all alone
And never friend come in or poor man stop.

God grant that I may live upon this earth
And face the tasks which every morning brings
And never lose the glory and the worth
Of humble service and the simple things.

It Couldn't Be Done

Somebody said that it couldn't be done
But he with a chuckle replied
That "maybe it couldn't," but he would be one
Who wouldn't say so till he'd tried.
So he buckled right in with the trace of a grin
On his face. If he worried he hid it.
He started to sing as he tackled the thing
That couldn't be done, and he did it!

Somebody scoffed: "Oh, you'll never do that;
At least no one ever has done it;"
But he took off his coat and he took off his hat
And the first thing we knew he'd begun it.
With a lift of his chin and a bit of a grin,
Without any doubting or quiddit,
He started to sing as he tackled the thing
That couldn't be done, and he did it.

There are thousands to tell you it cannot be done,
There are thousands to prophesy failure,
There are thousands to point out to you one by one,
The dangers that wait to assail you.
But just buckle in with a bit of a grin,
Just take off your coat and go to it;
Just start in to sing as you tackle the thing
That "cannot be done," and you'll do it.

As It Is

I might wish the world were better,
I might sit around and sigh
For a water that is wetter
And a bluer sort of sky.

There are times I think the weather
Could be much improved upon,
But when taken altogether
It's a good old world we're on.
I might tell how I would make it,
But when I have had my say
It is still my job to take it
As it is, from day to day.

I might wish that men were kinder,
And less eager after gold;
I might wish that they were blinder
To the faults they now behold.
And I'd try to make them gentle,
And more tolerant in strife
And a bit more sentimental
O'er the finer things of life.
But I am not here to make them,
Or to work in human clay;
It is just my work to take them
As they are from day to day.

Here's a world that suffers sorrow,
Here are bitterness and pain,
And the joy we plan to-morrow
May be ruined by the rain.
Here are hate and greed and badness,
Here are love and friendship, too,
But the most of it is gladness
When at last we've run it through.
Could we only understand it
As we shall some distant day
We should see that He who planned it
Knew our needs along the way.

Defeat

No one is beat till he quits,
No one is through till he stops,
No matter how hard Failure hits,
No matter how often he drops,
A fellow's not down till he lies
In the dust and refuses to rise

Fate can slam him and bang him around,
And batter his frame till he's sore,
But she never can say that he's downed
While he bobs up serenely for more.
A fellow's not dead till he dies,
Nor beat till no longer he tries.

Compensation

I'd like to think when life is done
That I had filled a needed post.
That here and there I'd paid my fare
With more than idle talk and boast;
That I had taken gifts divine.
The breath of life and manhood fine,
And tried to use them now and then
In service for my fellow men.

I'd hate to think when life is through
That I had lived my round of years
A useless kind, that leaves behind
No record in this vale of tears;
That I had wasted all my days
By treading only selfish ways,

And that this world would be the same
If it had never known my name.

I'd like to think that here and there,
When I am gone, there shall remain
A happier spot that might have not
Existed had I toiled for gain;
That someone's cheery voice and smile
Shall prove that I had been worth while;
That I had paid with something fine
My debt to God for life divine.

Chapter 10

Nature

Edgar Guest often wrote of his love of nature and his desire to spend time among it in his poetry. This poetry appeals to many because he conveys a nearly universal desire to spend time in the great outdoors.

Many people feel the urgency Edgar expressed when he wrote, "I must get out to the woods again." Being among the trees, feeling a warm breeze, or watching the neighborhood birds induces a sense of peace. Perhaps nature offers us this peace because God created both the world we enjoy and the peace we feel when we appreciate His creations.

Edgar's poetry aptly portrayed this yearning to be close to God by enjoying His creations.

Picture Books

I hold the finest picture books
Are woods an' fields an' running brooks;
An' when the month o' May has done
Her paintin', an' the morning sun
Is lightin' just exactly right
Each gorgeous scene for mortal sight,
I steal a day from toil an' go
To see the springtime's picture show.

It's everywhere I choose to tread—
Perhaps I'll find a violet bed
Half hidden by the larger scenes,
Or group of ferns, or living greens,
So graceful an' so fine, I'll swear
That angels must have placed them there

To beautify the lonely spot
That mortal man would have forgot.

What hand can paint a picture book
So marvelous as a runnin' brook?
It matters not what time o' day
You visit it, the sunbeams play
Upon it just exactly right,
The mysteries of God to light.
No human brush could ever trace
A droopin' willow with such grace!

Page after page, new beauties rise
To thrill with gladness an' surprise
The soul of him who drops his care
And seeks the woods to wander there.
Birds, with the angel gift o' song,
Make music for him all day long;

An' nothin' that is base or mean
Disturbs the grandeur of the scene.

There is no hint of hate or strife;
The woods display the joy of life,
An' answer with a silence fine
The scoffer's jeer at power divine.
When doubt is high an' faith is low,
Back to the woods an' fields I go,
An' say to violet and tree:
"No mortal hand has fashioned thee."

It's September

It's September, and the orchards are afire with red and gold,
And the nights with dew are heavy, and the morning's sharp with cold;
Now the garden's at its gayest with the salvia blazing red
And the good old-fashioned asters laughing at us from their bed;
Once again in shoes and stockings are the children's little feet,
And the dog now does his snoozing on the bright side of the street.

It's September, and the cornstalks are as high as they will go,
And the red cheeks of the apples everywhere begin to show;
Now the supper's scarcely over ere the darkness settles down
And the moon looms big and yellow at the edges of the town;
Oh, it's good to see the children, when their little prayers are said,
Duck beneath the patchwork covers when they tumble into bed.

It's September, and a calmness and a sweetness seem to fall
Over everything that's living, just as though it hears the call

Of Old Winter, trudging slowly, with his pack of ice and snow,
In the distance over yonder, and it somehow seems as though
Every tiny little blossom wants to look its very best
When the frost shall bite its petals and it droops away to rest.

It's September! It's the fullness and the ripeness of the year;
All the work of earth is finished, or the final tasks are near,
But there is no doleful wailing; every living thing that grows,
For the end that is approaching wears the finest garb it knows.
And I pray that I may proudly hold my head up high and smile
When I come to my September in the golden afterwhile.

Down the Lanes of August

Down the lanes of August—and the bees upon the wing,
All the world's in color now, and all the song birds sing;
Never reds will redder be, more golden be the gold,
Down the lanes of August, and the summer getting old.

Mother Nature's brushes now with paints are dripping wet,
Gorgeous is her canvas with the tints we can't forget;
Here's a yellow wheat field—purple asters there,
Riotous the colors that she's splashing everywhere.

Red the cheeks of apples and pink the peaches' bloom,
Redolent the breezes with the sweetness of perfume;
Everything is beauty crowned by skies of clearest blue,
Mother Earth is at her best once more for me and you.

Down the lanes of August with her blossoms at our feet,
Rich with gold and scarlet, dripping wet with honey sweet.
Rich or poor, no matter, here are splendors spread
Down the lanes of August, for all who wish to tread.

The Wide Outdoors

The rich may pay for orchids rare, but, Oh the apple tree
Flings out its blossoms to the world for every eye to see,
And all who sigh for loveliness may walk beneath the sky
And claim a richer beauty than man's gold can ever buy.

The blooming cherry trees are free for all to look upon;
The dogwood buds for all of us, and not some favorite one;
The wide outdoors is no man's own; the stranger on the street
Can cast his eyes on many a rose and claim its fragrance sweet.

Small gardens are shut in by walls, but none can wall the sky,
And none can hide the friendly trees from all who travel by;
And none can hold the apple boughs and claim them for his own,
For all the beauties of the earth belong to God alone.

So let me walk the world just now and wander far and near;
Earth's loveliness is mine to see, its music mine to hear;
There's not a single apple bough that spills its blooms about
But I can claim the joy of it, and none can shut me out.

The Call of the Woods

I must get out to the woods again, to the whispering trees and the birds awing,
Away from the haunts of pale-faced men, to the spaces wide where strength is king;
I must get out where the skies are blue and the air is clean and the rest is sweet,
Out where there's never a task to do or a goal to reach or a foe to meet.

I must get out on the trails once more that wind through shadowy haunts and cool,
Away from the presence of wall and door, and see myself in a crystal pool;
I must get out with the silent things, where neither laughter nor hate is heard,
Where malice never the humblest stings and no one is hurt by a spoken word.

Oh, I've heard the call of the tall white pine, and heard the call of the running brook;
I'm tired of the tasks which each day are mine; I'm weary of reading a printed book.
I want to get out of the din and strife, the clang and clamor of turning wheel,
And walk for a day where life is life, and the joys are true and the pictures real.

Poems

A Boy and His Dad 32

A Child of Mine 76

A Cup of Tea 58

A Friend's Greeting 116

A Package of Seeds 97

As It Is 134

A Song 81

A Warm House and a Ruddy Fire 88

Baby Feet 35

Be a Friend 122

Bulb Planting Time 98

Compensation 136

Daddies 45

Defeat 136

Down the Lanes of August 142

Failures 128

Friends 118

Grass and Children 85

Home 90

Home and the Office 43

I'll Never Be Rich 55

It Couldn't Be Done 134

It's September 140

Kindness 123

Little Feet 30

Living Beauties 96

Marjorie 79	Stick to It 128
Money 53	Story Telling 36
Mother's Job 37	Success 118
No Children! 38	The Call of the Woods 145
Now and Then 54	The Fellowship of Books 119
Our Little House 93	The Few 125
Picture Books 138	The Gentle Gardener 126
Questions 39	The Happy Slow Thinker 129
Results and Roses 127	The Home Builders 84
Reward 124	The Home-Wrecker 88
Rich 41	The Kindly Neighbor 114
She Mothered Five 46	The Making of a Friend 121
Silence 100	The Man I'm For 52
Since Jessie Died 78	The Obligation of Friendship 114

The Painter. 50	Troubles. 52
The Path to Home 82	Until She Died 80
The Simple Things. 133	What I Call Living. 130
The Spirit of the Home 42	When Day Is Done 94
The Test 120	When Pa Comes Home 44
The Things They Mustn't Touch 91	When Sorrow Comes 99
The Toy-Strewn Home. 87	Wife o' Mine. 57
The Way to Make Friends. 113	
The Wide Outdoors. 143	
Think Happy Thoughts. 131	
Tied Down 40	
To an Old Friend. 115	
To the Boy. 34	
Treasures. 95